When The Storks Flew South

DECISIONS THAT CHANGED HISTORY

DERICK BINGHAM

AMBASSADOR

When The Storks Flew South
© 1995 Derick Bingham

ISBN 1 898787 52 2

Published by

AMBASSADOR PRODUCTIONS, LTD.
16 Hillview Avenue,
Belfast, BT5 6JR

Emerald House Group, Inc.
1 Chick Springs Road, Suite 102
Greenville, South Carolina, 29609

Dwell on the past and you'll lose an eye.
Ignore the past and you'll lose both of them.

Old Russian Proverb

To Manus and Jane who created 'Randal's'
where hundreds of us have an unbelievably delicious scone
and coffee between making life's decisions!

Contents

Preface 7

When The Storks Flew South 11

Is That All? 19

Doers With Dreams 31

For Want Of Glasses 39

The Wandering Microbe 51

Dislike Of The Unlike 63

Two Hearts Beating Each To Each 81

The Greatest Decision Of All 99

The Three Lights 115

Bibliography 135

Preface

**If you don't make your own decisions
others will make them for you.**

DECISONS. DECISIONS. WE ALL HAVE TO MAKE THEM. IN FACT A RECENT STUDY CONCLUDED THAT ALL OF US FACE BETWEEN 300 AND 17,000 DECISIONS EVERY DAY.

Decisions, of course, have very far reaching repercussions. When President Truman made the decision to have a hydrogen bomb dropped on Hiroshima and Nagasaki over 300,000 people died in the aftermath. Yet when once pressed by a young political scientist, Truman maintained he had never lost any sleep over any decision he had to make. The wife of the Roman Prefect of Judea certainly had her sleep disturbed by a dream concerning the Galilean teacher her husband was trying in the Praetorium at Jerusalem. She tried to persuade Pontius Pilate to have nothing to do with "this just man" but he decided to have Jesus Christ crucified. It turned out to be a decision with incalculable results.

There are, though, a lot of people who are so afraid of being wrong in their decisions that they never get anything significant done in their lives. Former President Reagan learned the need for decision making early in life. An aunt had taken him to a cobbler's to have a pair of shoes made for him.

"Do you want a square toe or a round toe?" asked the cobbler. Reagan hummed and hawed. So the cobbler said, "Come back in a day or two and let me know what you want". A few days later the shoemaker saw Reagan on the street and asked what he had decided about the shoes. "I still haven't made up my mind", the boy answered. "Very well", said the cobbler. When Reagan received the shoes he was shocked to see that one shoe had a square toe and the other had a round toe. "Looking at those shoes every day taught me a lesson", said Reagan, years later, "If you don't make your own decisions somebody else will make them for you".

This book traces some of the more famous decisions in history. From Sir Alexander Fleming's decision to investigate bacteria to Abraham

Lincoln's decision to speak at Gettysburg: from Wilbur and Orville Wright's decision to investigate human flight to the decision of the men on the bridge of the R.M.S. TITANIC to ignore the need for the ship's lookouts to have access to a pair of binoculars, the variety of decision making was immense, yet the repercussions were, in all cases, mind-bending.

From Hitler's decision to wipe out all the Jews in Europe to Elizabeth Barrett's decision to marry the poet Robert Browning, to Napoleon Boneparte's decision to ignore the coming winter as storks flew over the head of his advancing army, I have sought to see what drove these people to make their decisions. I am, of course, aware that the Sovereign God has made us people, not puppets. Yet, it is difficult to know how much of decision making is up to us and how much of it leans upon Divine guidance. The problem, for me, has been delightfully summed up by the great Victorian preacher, C. H. Spurgeon. He said, "It is a difficult task to show the meeting place of the purpose of God and the free agency of man. One thing is quite clear, we ought not to deny either of them, for they are both facts. It is a fact that God has purposed all things both great and little; neither will happen but according to His eternal purpose and decree. It is also a sure and certain fact that oftentimes events hang upon the choice of men and women. How these two things can both be true I cannot tell you; neither probably after long debate could the wisest person in Heaven tell you, not even with the consistence of cherubim and seraphim .... they are true facts that run side by side, like parallel lines .... can you not believe them both? And is not the space between them a very convenient place to kneel in, adoring and worshipping Him whom you cannot understand?" I am aware that not all of the decision makers whom I have investigated would have followed Spurgeon's advice. It is my prayer, though, that after reading this book many of my readers will.

Derick Bingham
Belfast.
Summer of 1995

When The Storks Flew South

Napoleon Bonaparte's decision to march on Moscow despite what the storks told him.

IT WAS NOT AN EASY DECISION. IN APRIL 1812, THE EMPEROR OF ALL THE RUSSIAS, THE TSAR ALEXANDER, THE BLUE-EYED, CURLY HAIRED, SHY, BOYISH SON OF A BEAU-TIFUL MOTHER ISSUED AN ULTIMATUM TO NAPOLEON BONA-PARTE.

The Tzar had once been under the charm of the Emperor of the French, for, when he wanted to be charming, Napoleon could be just that. At noon on June 25th 1807, Napoleon was rowed out to a tented raft in the middle of the River Niemen, at Tilsit. Under the striped and bepennoned canvas the Tsar was waiting for him. Their separate armies watched from either bank as the two men embraced. In the following days they moved in what was the most exclusive club in the world. By July 7th they signed the Trea-ties of Tilsit, carving up Eastern Europe from the Baltic to the Bosphorous. The alliance between the two Emperors, though, had not lasted a full five years. Under huge pressure from his family, his court, and his nobles, the Tsar was persuaded to abandon his alliance with the "Corsican Corporal". His nobles charged him with being a traitor and very slowly he began to give way to their views. This pressure was summed up in his 1812 ultima-tum; "Napoleon must evacuate his troops from Prussia and the Grand Duchy of Warsaw as a preliminary to a new settlement of the frontiers of Europe."

Napoleon was now faced with a very difficult choice: he did not want to make war with Russia but the Poles wanted to remain within his Em-pire and the Grand Duchy was, in his view, essential to lasting peace across Europe. Napoleon decided that immediate war was the lesser of two evils. He now began to organise one of the most gigantic military operations in all history. For months on end troops poured into Prussia and the Grand Duchy of Warsaw; the assembly areas for the invasion of Russia. There were Swiss and Spanish, Portugese and Croats, Danish and Polish, Italian, Saxon and Dutch soldiers. In all, twenty nations and five hundred and thirty thousand men. The Grand Army, as it was called, consisted of a main strike force of four hundred and fifty thousand men. All of the planning and organisation of this huge army was tackled by Napoleon's brain, alone. His subordinates just did what he told them. "I will have", he directed his Director of War Administration, "Twenty million rations of bread ..... two million bushels of oats". He realised there would be nothing to hope for from the hostile Russian territory he would pass through and that his army would have to carry everything with them.

On July 24th 1812, where he had first embraced Alexander five years before, Napoleon stood and watched his Grand Army cross the River Niemen. It took his men eight days to cross the three pontoon bridges. Each division was followed by a six mile column of food supplies, live cattle, wagons of wheat, masons to build ovens and bakers to turn the wheat into bread. There were twenty-eight million bottles of wine and two million bottles of brandy. There were one thousand, one hundred and forty-six guns and over two thousand ammunition wagons. There were ambulances, stretchers, field dressings, bridging equipment and portable forges. There were thirty thousand wagons and carts and one hundred and fifty thousand horses.

Napoleon travelled in a green four-wheeled covered carriage drawn by six limousin horses. Inside the carriage were locked drawers which held his maps and reports. A lantern showed him working far into the night. It is a fact that Napoleon travelled so fast that when his sweating horses were changed at relays, buckets of water had to be poured over the smoking hot wheels. In the heart and psyche of one of the greatest military leaders in history there was, though, a deep seated flaw. Napoleon was an impatient man. When faced with a decision it is often best to be cautious and a swift, decisive move down a particular road can often be a disaster.

He was faced with a country vaster than he imagined: a country that had swallowed up Charles XIIth's Army in 1709 and destroyed it. But Napoleon had to be doing: "I act, therefore I am". Napoleon's ceaseless activity, as Correlli Barnett has pointed out "disguised the essential emptiness of his existence, the void in his heart". From a military standpoint it certainly would have been better if Napoleon had advanced step by step into Russia, conquering Province by Province and using these as a bargaining counter when he later sued for peace. This, of course, was never Napoleon's approach. He was always one for making a rapid swoop, fighting a great and victorious battle and then making peace. He had organised supplies for only three week's marching and the rapid swoop and victorious battle was the only way he could hope to defeat the Tsar. Napoleon was in a great hurry. As the smoking wheels of his carriage showed, he was in no condescending mood to stop for a moment and observe the flights of storks passing over his fated battalions. These huge birds knew that something was coming which was to be feared more than great armies or clever Generals; the Russian winter.

When it came it not only gripped the lakes and rivers, the hills and valleys and mountains, the hamlets and cities but it could freeze the breath of a man's mouth on his lips, form icicles under his nose and on his eyebrows and around his eyelids. It could, in fact, kill. It was not that Napoleon was unaware of the perils of the Russian winter. It was that he played fast and loose with it. When he reached Moscow he was to begin reading Voltaire's history of Charles XII in which the Swedish King tried to defy the Russian winter and saw, first, his horses die in the snow and then hundreds of his men. But Napoleon must move on. He must be active. He had to control events. On the way to Moscow the Grand Army fought and won the battle of Borodino, immortalised by the great novelist Tolstoy in "War and Peace", through the eyes of Prince Andre. The Russian losses at Borodino in dead and wounded were forty-four thousand men and the French losses were thirty-three thousand men. On the 15th September 1812 Napoleon entered Moscow, the city of onion domes and towers wearing the plain dark green uniform of a Colonel in the Chasseurs. One of Napoleon's Generals described how "The entire Army clapped its hands and repeated with rapture; 'Moscow! Moscow!' as sailors cry out 'Land! Land!' at the end of a long and hazardous voyage ..... Napoleon himself hurried forward.

He stopped in excitement; a cry of happiness escaped him .... 'There at last is this famous city! ..... and about time!'" The rapture of Napoleon and his army was to be short lived. Two hundred and thirty-five thousand of the inhabitants of Moscow had been ordered by the city's Governor to leave. Only fifteen thousand people were left including beggars and criminals and foreigners. Napoleon took up lodging in the Kremlin but no-one brought him the keys of the city as they had done over the years in Turin, Milan, Cairo, Vienna and Berlin. No huge crowds had watched him ride in. The city was, more or less, an empty prize. And worse was to come.

That night Moscow was torched. Over the next four days eight thousand five hundred homes were destroyed, four-fifths of the city of Moscow was a charred ruin. Count Rostopchin had armed a thousand convicts with fuses and gunpowder and ordered them to burn Moscow to the ground. This was a crossroads for Napoleon. He was faced with a decision, the results of which were to deeply affect history. On October 15th three inches of snow fell across the acres of charred and stinking debris and the facades of burnt-out buildings. Snow was an ominous forerunner of the deadly winter that would soon grip the Russias. He must make up his mind either to winter it out in Moscow or leave without a moment's delay. His subordinates urged him, if he were going to retreat, to do it while there was still time.

Vincent Cronin, the distinguished biographer, has made a very strong claim that Napoleon's great flaw of impatience expressed itself in his desire to control events. Napoleon had written to the Tsar who was in St. Petersburg on the 20th October trying to open peace talks. Since no reply had been received, his first idea was to march on St. Petersburg. He soon dropped this idea and then proposed a withdrawal West. He consulted Russian almanacs for the past twenty-five years and found the severe frosts came to the latitude of Moscow at the end of November. He reckoned that as the journey out had taken almost twelve weeks, presumably the journey back would take as long. If he was to go then he must leave immediately. Yet, he still held back, hoping to have a word from the Tsar. It proved to be his undoing. On the 18th October he finally gave his Grand Army the order to leave Moscow. At 2 p.m. in the afternoon of the 19th October his Army began to pull out. Ninety thousand infantry, fifteen thousand cavalry, five hundred and sixty-nine canon and ten thousand wagons with food for twenty days made a great spectacle.

Napoleon had, though, only provided horse fodder for less than one week deciding that the riders would do the foraging for food when needed. It was false optimism and foolhardy. He was playing around with the facts the storks had shown him weeks beforehand. On the 6th November there was twenty-two degrees of frost. Snow began to fall obliterating the sight of men from men. The army was harassed by Cossacks who prowled the flanks and rear of the army, picking off the sick, the exhausted and the straggler at the slightest opportunity. The horses, unprovided with frost nails, slipped in droves on the frozen mud, many so exhausted that they could not rise again and many breaking their legs. Napoleon himself shook with cold as though with an ague. It was so cold that at dawn men would disembowel horses that had died in the night and crawl inside to keep warm. Pressed by two armies sweeping in to attack, Napoleon could not now winter at Smolensk towards which he had been retreating. He eventually arrived at the Beresina River finding its bridge burned and under heavy Russian fire. He was now outnumbered three to one. Even in this incredible situation his military genius did not desert him. He had gained information from a peasant that an unmarked ford lay five miles up river.

He immediately sent a detachment six miles down river and ordered them to fell trees as though they were going to build a bridge. The Russian General Tchitchagov drew off all of his troops to the South, to

Napoleon's great elation. Napoleon could hardly believe his trick had worked.

The scene which followed, is, in the annals of military history, one of the bravest soldiers ever executed. Four hundred pontooners went into the icy waters and built two bridges over twenty-four hours. Practically every one of the pontooners died as a result of the operation. The first eleven thousand men had passed over by the time General Tchitchagov had realised his mistake. He now attacked with thirty-thousand men. It was a frightening sight but against huge odds and with the great courage of General Oudinot and General Ney in holding the bridgehead against the Russians, more than forty-thousand men crossed the Beresina.

Information had reached Napoleon while on his Russian campaign that a General Malet had published, with false documents, the announcement of Napoleon's death and tried to stage a coup in France. Napoleon felt he must get back to Paris quickly before the news of the Russian campaign disaster burst upon his Empire and putting his army under the care of General Murat, he left for home on the 5th December by sleigh.

Napoleon arrived in Warsaw four days later. He slipped undetected into the Hotel D'Angleterre and sent for the French Ambassador. In all his life the Ambassador never dreamt he would view the sight that met him. The man who was feted by kings was in a mean little, low- ceilinged hotel room with a maid servant kneeling by the chimney trying to unsuccessfully get flames from a greenwood fire. "From the sublime to the ridiculous is only a step", said the Emperor as he received his Ambassador and two Polish Ministers. For three hours he talked. "I couldn't prevent it freezing", he said. Indeed he couldn't but his impatience had made him disregard reality. "The fine weather tricked me", he said. "If I had set out a fortnight sooner, my army would be at Vitebsk". Truth was he should have wintered in Moscow but his flaw of impatience was, as happens to most who have it, un-noticed by himself. He lived to fight another day but it was the beginning of the end. Napoleon's retreat from Moscow was the turning point of his life and a turning point in the history of Europe. He once said of his army that "Movement alone keeps it together. One can advance at the head of it but neither stop nor retreat". Such a truth also applied to his Empire. Constant movement may have accounted for his success but it was to bring his final undoing. Sometimes the best decision to make when faced with a crisis is the decision to wait but the Emperor of the French couldn't wait. The storks were, by now, safe and well.

Is That All?

President Lincoln's decision to use 272 words at Gettysburg to remake America.

THE SCENE AT GETTYSBURG WAS ALL THAT CIVIL WAR ENTAILS. IT REPRESENTED A NATION TEARING ITSELF APART.

Two great armies, Union and Confederate had fumbled toward each other "like a pair of sidling crabs" and were now moving to lock in deadly battle at the quiet little town of Gettysburg in Pennsylvania with its population of only 2,500.

Eventually, for two days, July 1-2 the fighting raged and now, on the eve of July 2nd, along a ridge that ran south from the Gettysburg Cemetery, regiments and batteries were being slowly moved into position and ready for a final battle.

Who can chronicle the thoughts that must have run through minds and hearts that night? Pre-battle thoughts are thoughts which are wonderfully pared of all the trivia and nonsense that human beings spend their days worrying about. It is at such a time that men begin to understand and know what is truly valuable. The flickering lanterns, the Bible reading (next to dentures, Bibles were the most numerous of personal effects collected as the battle field was cleared), the mist; it was a sombre evening and a soul-searching night.

July 3rd dawned and as the sun rose it was the portent of a stiflingly hot day. The blast of 100 Confederate cannon enjoined the battle and for two hours the guns from both Armies spat death across the valley. Then the firing lulled. A huge mass of men dressed in grey began to surge out of the woods as General Lee threw 15,000 men into a massed assault. The wave of grey came on and on, eventually becoming a blue and grey swirling, fighting mass. The battle hung in the balance for a moment and then the grey wave broke and began to retreat back down the slope and across the valley. As it retreated, Union guns blasted into it.

When darkness eventually fell the aftermath that lay across the battle-field at Gettysburg was devastating. "It had been the most thundering cannonading and grimly appalling loss of lives on both sides that had ever occurred in the Western hemisphere", wrote Reinhard Luthin. The Union Army lost 23,000 men out of 93,000 engaged and the Confederate Army around 30,000 out of 70,000.

Pickett's Division alone lost 3,392 of its 4,500 men including all Commanders of Brigades and Regiments. "For seven days", wrote one nurse, "the tables ran with blood". Preachers quoted the 23rd Psalm as fast as their lips could say it over dying soldiers.

For a disagreeable length of time the bodies from the three-day carnage lay openly or only hastily half buried at Gettysburg. The scene was repellent. Householders had to plant around bodies in their fields and gardens or remove the decaying bodies themselves. Relatives arrived and rifled the many graves, looking for their dead and re-burying the other bodies they turned up even more hastily than the first disposal crews, with arms, legs and heads protruding.

The situation could not be allowed to remain unattended. People began to demand a specially dedicated burial ground and eventually the Governors of 18 Northern States appointed Trustees to establish a new cemetery. The Government of Pennsylvania appointed the 32 year old Gettysburg Civil Leader, David Wills, to be in charge on the scene. Wills formed an Inter-State Commission to collect funds for the cleansing of fields at Gettysburg. The Federal Government shipped in thousands of coffins and Wills took title to 17 acres for the new cemetery. A Scotsman called William Saunders created the cemetery's layout, arranging graves in great curving ranks, State by State, with no State receiving preference over another.

As the work proceeded Wills now felt "the need for artful words to sweeten poisoned air". But who would speak such words? He approached the poets of the day, Longfellow, Whittier and Bryant but they did not rise to the occasion. An orator was needed, someone who could lift the whole ghastly scene to some wider, broader picture and give it purpose and meaning at a dedication ceremony.

The choice fell upon the man reckoned to be the greatest living orator in America, Edward Everett. Unitarian Minister, Harvard Professor of Greek Literature, Editor, Orator, Poet, five term Republican Congressman, four term Governor of Massachusetts, United States Minister to England, President of Harvard College, United States Secretary of State, United States Senator and, in 1860, candidate for the Vice Presidency of the United States, Edward Everett was a very distinguished gentleman by any count.

It seems incredible, though, in the light of history that the Commander-in-chief of the Union Army, President Abraham Lincoln, was only casually invited to Gettysburg two months after Everett was invited. The President had earlier made known his intention to attend and, it would seem, the organisers, out of sympathy, asked him to deliver "a few appropriate remarks". They meant no insult to the President but it was privately thought he "would not be able to speak upon such a great and solemn occasion as that of the Memorial Services". It was a very ironical prelude to one of the greatest speeches in world history. Lincoln took no offence but he did take his "few appropriate remarks" very seriously indeed. That he was, when the moment came, able to raise himself so magnificently to the occasion is one of the great deeds of history.

Lincoln's Gettysburg address is revered by millions today, but, when the cauldron of emotion in which it was formed is studied in detail, it is just incredible that he towered above his circumstances to couch democracy in its most memorable phrase and to inspire millions.

Consider Lincoln's circumstances, even his immediate circumstances. As General Lee and his troops retreated from Gettysburg towards the River

Potomac, the War Department rushed 20,000 fresh troops to General Meade and Lincoln urged him to follow up the victory at Gettysburg with a "stunning blow" before he crossed the river. Lee, in fact, had reached the Potomac and found it swollen with heavy rains and was trapped. For a whole week General Meade held back. "He was within your easy grasp and to have closed upon him would, in connection with our other late successes, have ended the war", wrote Lincoln in a letter to Meade which he never sent.

While Meade had waited the river subsided and the Confederate forces had built bridges and, under the cover of darkness on July 13th, they had crossed the river and slipped away. "The war will be prolonged indefinitely", wrote the deeply disappointed Lincoln. Meade had congratulated his Army on winning at Gettysburg and "driving the enemy from our soil". "Will our Generals never get that idea out of their heads?", said Lincoln, "The whole country is our soil". Meade's indecision, though, was not Lincoln's only hassle. On July 2nd his wife was travelling in a carriage in Washington when the driver's seat became detached from the rest of Mrs. Lincoln's carriage. The driver was thrown out, the horses bolted and the First Lady was tossed upon the ground striking her head against a sharp rock.

Mary Lincoln's condition, though, had long been a deep worry and concern to the President. In February 1862 the President's very promising son, Willie, suddenly took ill with a fever and died. On a windy day, with roofs being blown off houses the President drove "unseeing through the wreckage" to his son's funeral. Mental illness invaded Mary Lincoln's life and no wonder. From a Confederate "high society" family in Bluegrass, Kentucky, Mary's favourite half-brother Alec had fallen in battle at Baton Rouge, another half-brother Sam had been killed leading his Confederate command at Shiloh and a third half-brother was killed at the Battle of Vicksburg. The husband of her favourite half-sister was trampled to death in the slaughter at Chickamauga.

Poor Lincoln; he who had faced opposition from Mary's family when he first fell in love with her because they felt he had come from "nowhere", namely that he was a coarse man of Indiana backwoods origin and "poor purse", now decided to allow his wife's widowed sister-in- law to come and stay at the White House. He sent a message through the Union lines to bring her from the South and he was, of course, then accused of harbouring a rebel. Mary had long been snubbed by her own family because she was the wife of a "black Republican President". The agonies of Civil War came right into the White House. Willie's death, of course, had long affected Lincoln just as deeply as it had Mary though he managed to cover his feelings by an outwardly pleasant self. Any President's load is heavy but for Lincoln, particularly in the four years of seemingly unending war from 1861-65, it must have verged on the virtually unendurable.

As the time for the Gettysburg dedication approached , Lincoln was scheduled to leave Washington on the morning of the 19th of November reaching Gettysburg via Baltimore. It was intended that after he had delivered his short speech he should return to Washington at 6 o'clock the same evening. Lincoln vetoed the proposed schedule, saying "I do not wish to so go that by the slightest accident we fail entirely and at best the whole be a mere breathless running of the gauntlet". So, on November 18th, ensuring an uninterrupted arrival at the dedication ceremony, Lincoln left a very sick son, Tad, with his very worried and frightened wife at the White House. Destiny, though, was calling and Lincoln meant business as his train steamed into Gettysburg at sundown.

Thousands of people thronged the little town. A harvest moon was up and a military band played in the square near Mr. David Wills' home where the President was a guest. He sat down to dinner with the orator Everett and various European diplomats and American dignitaries. A crowd gathered outside the Wills' house and the Fifth New York Artillery serenaded the President. He thanked them and said he had no speech to make, commenting, "In my position it is somewhat important that I should not say foolish things". "Not if you can help it", cried a heckler to which the President retorted, "It very often happens that the only way to help it is to say nothing at all. Believing that is my present condition this evening, I must beg you to excuse me from addressing you further". History is very glad that Lincoln did not remain as silent the next day for the English language was not to contain a better political speech than the modest, "Honest Abe" was to give.

Lincoln retired at around 10 o'clock. Telegrams reported all quiet on all fighting fronts and a telegram from Mrs. Lincoln reported that Tad felt better. The President now began to work on his speech, again making some revisions. "The few appropriate remarks" were taking shape and few realised in the crowds milling around in the street outside that the most famous delineation of democracy was taking shape in the lamplight of the President's room.

The mind and hand that wrote the Gettysburg address had come a long way since birth in the log cabin in Sinking Spring, Kentucky on February 12th, 1809. Later the family had moved and Lincoln had grown up in Pigeon Creek, Indiana and earned his first dollars as a ferryman on a flat-boat on the Ohio River dressed in "his deerskin shirt, his home-made jeans - breeches dyed brown with walnut bark, his coonskin cap crumpled in his big callused hands". In time he became a Postmaster and a local store owner and then after much study he qualified in law and showed, for 24 years, a real talent for advocacy as an Appeals Lawyer on the "Prairie Circuit". Eventually he entered politics and was as skilled at arousing a "stump audience" as in swaying judges and juries.

Politics was Lincoln's natural habitat and with all his other experiences on top of his political ones, the path leading to destiny's moment was fast approaching as the weary President made his speech revisions before sleeping. He was about, under God, to remake a nation.

Lincoln was a master of English prose. From his private letters to his public speeches, even from his handwritten State papers, there are plenty of literary gems. The hand that had just finished revising the speech of his life, and America's life, also wrote these tender words to the daughter of Lt. Col. McCullough who fell on a battlefield in Mississippi: "Dear Fanny, It is with deep grief that I learn of the death of your kind and brave father; and, especially, that it is affecting your young heart beyond what is common in such cases. In this sad world of ours, sorrow comes to all; and, to the young it comes with bitterest agony, because it takes them unawares. The older have learned to ever expect it. I am anxious to afford some alleviation of your present distress. Perfect relief is not possible, except with time. You cannot now realise that you will ever feel better. Is not this so?

And yet it is a mistake. You are sure to be happy again. To know this, which is certainly true, will make you less miserable now. I have had experience enough to know what I say; and you need only to believe it, to feel better at once. The memory of your dear father, instead of an agony, will yet be a sad sweet feeling in your heart, of a purer and holier sort than you have known before. Please present my kind regards to your afflicted mother. Your sincere friend, Abraham Lincoln".

It was such a man who led the long procession of mounted dignitaries at 10 o'clock the next morning, after the minute guns on Cemetery Heights had given warning of the solemn occasion that was to follow. He wore a mourning band on his hat for his dead son and white gauntlets.

The orator Everett had already gone out to prepare himself in a special tent erected for him near the platform (he had kidney trouble). Only one-third of the bodies had been buried at Gettysburg and graves were still being readied for bodies that arrived irregularly. Marshals had to keep the near 20,000 people out of the work in progress.

Everett rose to speak, placing a very thick text on a little table in front of him. He didn't need the text, though, for he had mastered all the arts of eloquence and always learned his speeches off by heart. He had studied the battlefield carefully pointing out, with gestures, the sights of the battle's progress, visible from where he stood as he spoke. He berated the rebels, some of whose bodies still lay unburied. He swayed the audience powerfully, with his detailed knowledge. His speech was brilliant, intellectually, but, was, as one observer said, "as cold as ice".

His voice was sweet and modulated and with the oratory of the Greek Revival, popular in academic circles in America at the time, he spoke for one hour and fifty-seven minutes. The speech was in no way counted boring by the thousands who heard it and appreciated it. As has been pointed out, the modern rock concert lasts at least three hours and people who like that sort of thing think nothing of it. Neither did Everett's audience, though restless, think any the less of him for his longevity.

At exactly 2 o'clock, in the words of one who was there, "the tall form of the President appeared on the stand and never before have I seen a crowd so vast and restless, after standing so long, so soon stifled and quiet. Hats were removed and all stood motionless to catch the first words he should utter".

His words were finished almost before some in the crowd knew he had started. His words were exactly 272 in total and took three minutes to deliver. When he sat down John Young of the "Philadelphia Press" whispered, "Is that all?". "Yes, that's all", Lincoln answered.

"The cheek of every American must tingle with shame", said the "CHICAGO TIMES", "As he reads the silly, flat, dishwatery utterances of the man who has to be pointed out to intelligent foreigners as the President of the United States". Silly? Flat? Dishwatery? The big daily newspapers of the United States printed Lincoln's speech inconspicuously in their papers. Even Lincoln made one glaringly inaccurate appraisal of his own speech when he said that "the world will little note, nor long remember what we say here". The world in fact has never forgotten what he said at Gettysburg. Time has immortalised his 272 words.

To be fair to Everett he wrote to the President that "I should be glad if I could flatter myself that I came near to the central idea of the occasion in two hours, as you did in two minutes".

What was it that made those 272 words so influential in history? What was it about it that remade a bitterly divided America? It was Lincoln's decision to use his speech to elevate the Declaration of Independence above the United States Constitution. Nowhere does the United States Constitution mention the powerful assertion that America was built on the "proposition that all men are created equal". It gave the Declaration of Independence a new position as America's founding document and then "put into words", as Ben McIntyre has stated, "The spirit of American nationhood, already in the hearts and minds of many". (The Times, July 14th, 1992). It damned slavery, an issue Lincoln had long wrestled with and it epitomised the importance of the people over big Government or dictators.

Gary Wills has argued that by introducing the principle of human equality as the founding proposition of American nationhood, Lincoln carried out "one of the most daring acts of open-air slight- off-hand ever witnessed by the unsuspecting. Everyone in that vast throng of thousands was having his or her intellectual pocket picked. The power of words has rarely been given a more compelling demonstration".

Lincoln's decision to go to Gettysburg and use his 272 words was, for the cause of democracy and human dignity, one of the most important decisions ever made. His "few appropriate remarks" could not, in history's light, have been more appropriate.

THE GETTYSBURG ADDRESS

November 19th, 1863

Four score and seven years ago our fathers brought forth on this Continent, a new nation. Conceived in Liberty, and dedicated to the proposition that all men are created equal.

Now we are engaged in a great Civil War, testing whether that nation, or any nation so conceived and so dedicated, can long endure. We are met on a great battlefield of that war. We have come to dedicate a portion of that field, as a final resting place to those who here gave their lives that that nation might live. It is altogether fitting and proper that we should do this.

But, in a larger sense, we can not dedicate - we can not consecrate - we can not hallow - this ground. The brave men, living and dead, who struggled here, have consecrated it, far above our poor power to add or detract. The world will little note, nor long remember what we say here, but it can never forget what they did here. It is for us the living, rather, to be dedicated here to the unfinished work which they who fought here have thus far so nobly advanced.

It is rather for us to be here dedicated to the great task remaining before us - that from these honoured dead we take increased devotion to that cause for which they gave the last full measure of devotion - that we here highly resolve that these dead shall not have died in vain - that this nation, under God, shall have a new birth of freedom - and that government of the people, by the people, for the people, shall not perish from the earth.

Abraham Lincoln.

Doers With Dreams

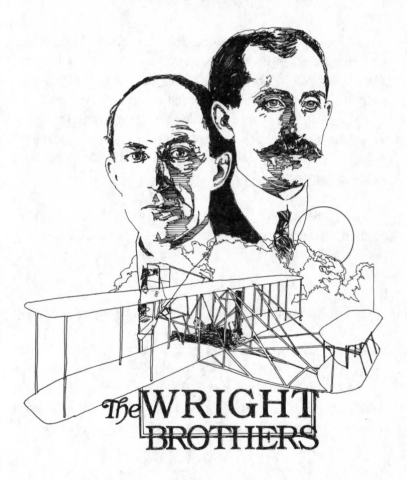

The Wright brothers' decision to investigate flight.

BISHOP MILTON WRIGHT LIVED IN CEDAR RAPIDS, IOWA WITH A SALARY OF LESS THAN ONE THOUSAND DOLLARS A YEAR. HIS WORK AS A MINISTER INVOLVED MUCH TRAVEL INTO THE HINTERLAND AND ONE DAY IN 1878 HE RETURNED FROM ONE OF HIS MANY TRIPS WITH A GIFT FOR HIS TWO YOUNGEST SONS, WILBUR AND ORVILLE.

Hardly concealing his gift in his hands the Bishop tossed it into the air before the lads could see what it was. It flew across the room to their utter delight. It was a toy helicopter made of cork, bamboo and paper and the twin propellors were activated by a twisted rubber band. Bishop Wright had no idea that when he tossed that little toy helicopter into the air that his two boys were one day to change history by inventing engine powered flight which was not only to turn the world into a neighbourhood but to take man to the moon.

In June 1884 Bishop Wright's family moved to Dayton, Ohio. A family friend, Ed Stines, persuaded Wilbur and his brother Lorden to trade their jointly owned homemade boat for a small printing press, which was presented to Orville.

The Bishop gave 25 lbs. of type as a gift. A four page school paper called 'THE MIDGET' was launched. When Wilber turned eighteeen he joined Orville in his work and with a larger press they published a weekly paper called 'THE WESTSIDE NEWS' which lasted for a year. It became 'THE EVENING ITEM' which lasted for only three months and expired in August 1890. Wilbur and Orville then set themselves up as Job Printers and moved to larger quarters printing calling cards and advertising leaflets.

Printing, though, was not to be the Wright Brother's destiny. By the 1890's the world of cycling had become a national obsession in the United States. The bicycle had evolved from a contraption with two huge front wheels with a rider perched four to five feet from the ground to a V-framed "safety bicycle" with a sprocket- chain drive, ballbearings, comfortable saddles and coaster brakes.

Orville and Wilbur decided to let Ed Stines run their printing business and opened a bicycle shop across the street. Little did they know it was to become the most famous bicycle shop in history. It was to be moved brick by brick along with the Wright family house on Hawthorn Street by the famous Henry Ford himself and reconstructed brick by brick and side by side at Henry Ford's Greenfield Village in Dearborn, Michican where it can be viewed today. In the summer of 1893 such an unimaginable event was not even in Wilbur and Orville's dreams. By 1895, however, they were manufacturing their own bicycles.

It is generally accepted by historians that Wilbur and Orville's first real interest in human flight was sparked by reading about the work of Otto Lilienthal, a German mechanical engineer. Otto was concerned that the solution to human flight would be found if man imitated the flapping flight of birds. He soon discarded this idea but over a six year period he built eighteen variations of a basic hang-glider. The most successful of these had a wing span of 25 feet, constructed so that the wings could be folded back like the wings of a bat. Sadly Wilbur and Orville read of "The Flying Man's" death on Sunday, August 9th 1896. Lilienthal was killed while gliding in the Rhinow Hills forty miles from Berlin.

The death of Lilienthal brought renewed interest in human flight to the minds of the Wright Brothers. Usually when their interest in a subject was sparked they looked it up in the encyclopaedia. They could find nothing on the subject of human flight in the encyclopaedias available in their own home library or even in the Dayton Public Library. The librarians at Dayton had no idea that the two brothers searching through the encyclopaedia on the shelves of the Dayton Public Library were soon to spawn innumerable books on human flight that continue to this day. It is worth noting that librarians are very important people and they should take great care of any enquirer. "Wilbur and I could hardly wait for morning to come", Orville reflected later, "To get at something that interested us. That's happiness". For three years the brothers' interest in human flight simmered and then one day they decided to do something about it.

On May 30th 1899 the citizens of Dayton were celebrating Decoration Day by decking the graves of the Civil War dead. Wilbur, though, decided to lift his pen and write a letter to Washington. On such seemingly small hinges do the great doors of history swing. The humble bicycle shop owner sitting at his sister's bandy legged desk in the parlour of a modest home in Ohio writing a letter does not seem, on the face of it, to have anything to do with a modern tornado jet screaming across a frontier sky or a giant 400 seater jet liner now approaching John F. Kennedy Airport in New York, or even with cosmonauts in a space station orbiting the earth. Yet, there in that humble parlour as the firm-faced, clefted-chinned, prominent-eared Wilbur Wright leaned over his letter was the seedbed of it all. The two brothers were, as Neil Armstrong, the first man on the moon put it, "Doers with dreams".

Wilbur was addressing his letter to the Secretary of the Smithsonian Institution in Washington, D.C. In it he expressed his faith in the feasibility of human flight and stated, "I am about to begin a systematic study of the subject in preparation for practical work to which I expect to devote what time I can spare from my regular business. I wish to obtain such papers as the Smithsonian Institution has published on this subject, and if possible, a list of other works in print in the English language".

Three days later the Institution replied with pamphlets and a list of books available commercially. Soon Wilbur and Orville were at work on a bi-plane of their own. Their genius soon began to emerge. One of the major problems faced was how to have lateral control, the kind a bird uses to produce a turn or to correct the rocking of its wings in soaring flight. Today we know modern aircraft achieve lateral control by moving the ailerons on the rear edges of the two wings in opposite directions. It all seems fairly obvious now, but, it was not at all obvious in 1899.

How could "wing-twisting" be achieved? One day the Wright Brothers were watching a flock of pigeons flying and on close observation they reckoned that a pigeon achieved lateral control by presenting one wing tip at a positive angle to its line of flight and the other at a negative angle. They reckoned that when the pigeon had revolved as far as it wished, it reversed the process and began to roll the other way. It didn't shift weight, its balance was simply controlled by utilising dynamic reactions of the air. How could such a thing be achieved in human flight?

It was Wilbur who stumbled on the solution. One summer's evening, when the bicycle shop was opened late, Wilbur was selling a tube for a bicycle tyre to a customer. Taking the tube out of its box he began to absent-mindedly twist the ends of the open box in opposite directions. It suddenly occurred to him that if a frail pasteboard box could survive such strain it might be possible to trust the cloth-covered wooden frame of a flying machine in the same fashion without sacrificing lateral stiffness. Wilbur took the box home, ripped the ends off and demonstrated its twisting propensities to Orville. They utilised this principle into their bi-plane. To effect lateral control they would merely twist the right and left wings in opposite directions.

Soon the brothers built a kite model and after experimenting on it decided it was time to try out their control system on a man-carrying glider. They calculated that they would need wind of between fifteen and sixteen miles an hour on fairly open ground to support their glider in flight and wrote to the Weather Bureau in Washington with such an experimental site in mind. The Weather Bureau sent back a copy of the "Monthly Weather Review" giving the average hourly winds at all Weather Bureau Stations in the United States. Going through the "Monthly Weather Review" Wilbur noted that winds of the strength required for their glider had been reported at Kitty Hawk, North Carolina. Wilbur wrote to the Weather Station at Kitty Hawk for more specific information. Back came a letter saying that the beach was about one mile wide, was clear of trees or high hills and extended for nearly sixty miles in the same condition. The letter informed the Wright Brothers that the wind blew mostly from the north and north east in September and October. They were informed that there was no house to rent in the area and that if they wanted to conduct their glider experiments, they had better bring tents. So it was at the village of Kitty Hawk, on the Outer Banks, a two hundred mile strip of sand that acts as a buffer between the ocean and the North Carolina mainland, was immortalised.

On September 6th, 1900 Wilbur set off for Kitty Hawk. By train, then by ferry, he eventually boarded a flat bottomed schooner owned by one Israel Perry. The rotting schooner was a disaster. Wilbur, with baggage, trunk and white pine spruce strips (bought for 7 dollars and 70 cents) to construct his glider, sailed from Manleo Roanoke Island, North Carolina for Kitty Hawk on the Outer Banks. He very nearly perished in a full blown gale and no more relieved individual ever arrived at what was an unlit and deserted wharf at Kitty Hawk, seven days after setting out from Dayton.

As Wilbur waited for Orville he could be seen splicing fine French sateur for wing coverings for the glider and although the citizens of Kitty Hawk were curious, they were sceptical. They believed that God did not intend that man should every fly!

Soon Orville joined Wilbur and they erected their tent, anchored to a gnarled oak and settled down to their work. The two men were to make regular trips between 1900-1903 to Kitty Hawk and were constantly beset by rain, thirst, sickness, sand fleas and mosquitos. "They chewed us clear through our underwear and socks", Orville wrote home. No mesh was fine enough to keep them out. Undaunted, the Wright Brothers pursued their dreams.

Eventually the Wright experiments settled at Kill Devil Hills, four miles from Kitty Hawk, particularly at Big Kill Devil Hill, sandwiched in the Outer Banks between Albermarle Sound and the Atlantic Ocean. It was here on the morning of December 17th, 1903 that the bicycle shop owners from Dayton, Ohio, shook the dust from history and turned the world into a neighbourhood. What they did on that momentous morning actually linked the yellow sands of Kitty Hawk with the gritty dust of the moon.

At 10:35 am Orville Wright, lying prone on the lower wing of what became known as "The Flyer" with sand hissing against its fabric and its engine with its banging roar, reached the end of its track at about thirty miles per hour. It flew an estimated one hundred and twenty feet in twelve seconds and it was described by Orville as "the first in the history of the world in which a machine carrying a man had raised itself by its own power into the air in full flight, had sailed forward without reduction of speed and had finally landed at a point as high as that from which it started." The Wright brothers actually made four flights on that day and there will always be controversy about which one of them actually deserves to be called the first in history. Some think it was Wilbur's accurately timed and measured fifty-nine second, eight hundred and fifty-two foot flight, the fourth of the day, that was the world's first sustained free flight with a man. Whoever did it first one thing is certain, between them they had conquered human flight.

Perhaps Bishop Wright had best summed up the relationship between his two sons. "They are," he wrote, "as inseparable as twins. For several years they have read up on aeronautics as a physician would read his books, and they have studied, discussed and experimented together. Natural workmen, they have invented, constructed and operated their gliders and finally their "Wright Flyer" jointly, all at their own personal expense. About equal credit is due each."

Wilbur Wright died on Wednesday 26th May, 1912 and an estimated 25,000 people passed by his open casket at the First Presbyterian Church at Dayton. Orville died on Friday 30th January, 1947. As they carried Orville's remains to the woodland cemetery, four jet fighters roared overhead in a five-plane formation. The fifth plane missing from its slot was the equivalent to the riderless horse in a full dress military funeral.

It was, as Orville put it, that drive, "to get to that which interests us" that brought about their great discovery. That letter from Washington to Wilbur explaining that he wanted all available data on human flight was a turning point in history. It shows us that we must never despise anyone's decision to make a humble attempt to thoroughly investigate something. It's a long journey from Kitty Hawk to the moon but those two humble bicycle shop owners made such a journey possible.

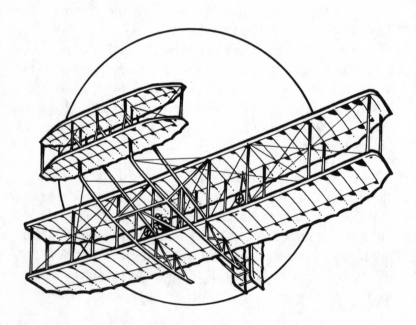

For Want Of Glasses

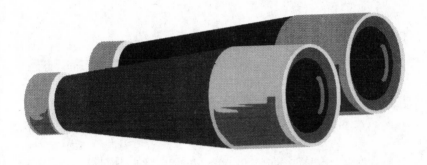

The decision of the chain of command on board the R.M.S. TITANIC to neglect giving binoculars to their lookouts on the night of April 14th, 1912.

SHE CARRIED 75,000 POUNDS OF FRESH MEAT AND 35,000 FRESH EGGS. THERE WERE, ON BOARD, 1,500 GALLONS OF FRESH MILK AND 40 TONS OF POTATOES.

There were also 800 bundles of fresh asparagus and 1,750 quarts of ice cream with 1,000 oyster forks, 4,500 breakfast cups, 2,000 egg spoons, 1,000 finger bowls, 400 toast racks, 10,000 pounds of cereals and 12,000 dinner plates. To keep any spillage off suits and dresses, there were 45,000 table napkins. Her manifest states that there were on board 3,500 pounds of tomatoes, 2,500 pounds of fresh green peas and 2,200 pounds of coffee, 15,000 bottles of ale and stout, 1,000 bottles of wine and 1,000 pounds of hothouse grapes, 25,000 pounds of poultry and 11,000 pounds of fresh fish.

In her cabins there were, altogether, 800 eiderdown quilts, 15,000 pillow slips, 15,000 single sheets, 7,500 bath towels, 7,500 blankets and 3,600 bed covers. In beauty and luxury she was unsurpassed. Some of her best cabins had full size four poster beds and Adam fireplaces that burned coal. The two grandest suites, 50 feet long, had private promenade decks.

There were electric lifts, a gymnasium with mechanical horses, a rackets court, a swimming pool, Turkish baths with shampoo-ing rooms and the Cafe Parisien, which was, wrote Sir Philip Gills, "a tropical verandah restaurant where vines grew upon the lattice work of windows, and where "at night the band played the best tunes of life". Every style of architecture was represented in the great ship; Elizabethan, Adam, Louise Quinze, Queen Anne, Dutch and Louis Quatoze. Many of the toilets were of costly marble. Her mirrors vied with those of Versailles, her first class stairway with that of the finest English country house.

Her gross tonnage of 46,328 tons made her the largest ship afloat. She was 882 feet long, 92 feet wide and had eight decks rising to the height of an eleven storey building. She was the brainchild of Lord W. J. Pirrie, a partner in the Belfast shipbuilding firm, Harland and Wolff, in partnership with the White Star Line. Lord Pirrie decided to build three monster ships to wipe out opposition on the Atlantic run which was hugely lucrative as emigration to the United States from Europe was, at that time, massive. The "homesick trade" back again was also lucrative and was at one stage at least 100,000 strong as disappointed or homesick Britons came home. The first monster ship was the OLYMPIC, the second the TITANIC, and the third, the BRITTANIC but it was the second ship which was to become, to the man in the street, the best known ship in all history.

The memory of the TITANIC simply refuses to go away. She is etched in people's minds to this day as a symbol. Even now she is used regularly by political cartoonists depicting the troubles of Presidents and Prime Ministers. People are endlessly fascinated by her. The list of passengers and crew who sailed on her maiden voyage are poured over and their social class and wealth or lack of it commented upon as epitomising the Edwardian life in which she was launched.

The passenger list included the name of Mrs. Charlotte Cardeza of Philadelphia who had on board 14 trunks, 4 suitcases, 3 crates and a medicine chest. They contained 70 dresses, 10 fur coats, 38 large feather pieces, 22 hat pins and 91 pairs of gloves. Another passenger, Mr. Billy Carter, also from Philadelphia, had a 35 horse power Renault on board, with 60 shirts, 15 pairs of shoes, 2 sets of tails and 24 polo sticks. Col. J. J. Astor, who built the Waldorf Astoria Hotel in New York, was also a passenger and was said to be worth $30 million. Another passenger, Mr. Benjamin Guggenheim was said to be worth $20 million and Mr. Isidor Strauz was declared to be worth $10 million.

It is interesting to reflect that the Second Wireless Operator, Mr. Harold Bride, made $20 a month. He would have had to spend 15 years salary to cross the Atlantic in the style of the first class passengers whose telegrams from ship to shore he constantly handled. How much less did the steerage passengers earn among whom were emigrating Syrians, Armenians, Irish and Italian passengers? What can we say of the salaries of the stokers managing the 159 furnaces and 29 boilers on board never to speak of the 14,000 men of Harland and Wolff who built the TITANIC for £2.00 a 49 hour week?

There were 2,227 passengers and crew on board when, after four days and seventeen hours into her maiden voyage from Southampton, the TITANIC hit an iceberg at 11.40 p.m. on Sunday, 10th April 1912. Two hours and forty minutes later she sank. Of her 2,227 passengers and crew, 705 escaped in 20 lifeboats and rafts and 1,522 were drowned with her Master Captain Edward Smith.

The RMS TITANIC was the pride of the nation when she glided down the slips into Belfast Lough on May 31st, 1911 lubricated with 3 tons of soft soap, 15 tons of tallow and 5 tons of tallow mixed with train oil. It was Lord Pirrie, the Chairman of Harland and Wolff's birthday and with the OLYMPIC already in the Lough waiting and ready to take his distinguished guests back to England, the White Star Line seemed poised on the edge of a new era. The TITANIC was already a legend even before she hit the water.

Her chosen master, Captain Edward Smith, a Southampton man had sailed 2 million miles for the White Star Line. He was the highest paid man afloat, the Commodore of the White Star Fleet. In 1906 when Captain Smith had brought the ADRIATIC across the Atlantic he had told the New York press that "when anyone asks me how I can best describe my experiences of nearly 40 years at sea, I merely say "uneventful". I have never been in any accident of any sort worth speaking about. I never saw a wreck and have never been wrecked, nor was I ever in any predicament that threatened to end in disaster of any sort".

He also added, "I cannot imagine any condition which would cause a ship to founder. I cannot conceive of any vital disaster happening to this vessel. Modern ship building has gone beyond that".

Many a sermon has been preached on Captain Smith's over confidence. He has been lambasted as the epitomy of man's unhealthy trust in technology and for presuming against God and nature. There is also a well attested fact that the TITANIC received at least six ice warnings on her maiden voyage. At 11 p.m. the steamer CALIFORNIAN suddenly broke in by wireless; "I say, old man, we are stopped and surrounded by ice". "Shut up, shut up", shot back First Wireless Officer Phillips, "I'm busy, I'm working Cape Race". Indeed he was. He was passing messages for passengers requesting hotel reservations, instructing business associates, giving arrival times that were never to materialise. The last message he received he put under a paper weight and forgot all about it.

In hindsight it now seems incredible that Captain Smith took the TITANIC into what proved to be an enormous belt of ice stretching some 78 miles directly across her path at 22 knots (i.e. 38 feet per second) after repeated serious warnings. We now baulk at the absolute trust in technology that proved so fatal when his gigantic command hit a granite hard iceberg 50 feet high weighing approximately 500,000 tons and at least 3,000 years old.

We are told that someone in the Belfast Shipyard scrawled on the side of the TITANIC, "Even Jesus Christ Himself couldn't sink this ship". Overweening pride that mocks God and His Christ is a very dangerous thing. The dangers of human presumption that thinks we can by technology overcome reality are still all around us. The strains of Wallace Hartley's band that played the hymn "Nearer my God to Thee" as the TITANIC sank into the calm and freezing waters of the Atlantic still reach us. They are worth heeding for, after all, what will it profit us to gain the whole world and lose our own souls? Nothing. One thing is certain; if man rests on technological hubris he will be humbled.

All human life and its foibles were epitomised as the TITANIC sank. There was bravery and there was skulduggery. There was sacrifice and there was selfishness. There was wisdom and there was foolishness.

As the boat was sinking Isidor Straus, the owner of Macy's famous rAstore in New York was offered a seat in a lifeboat. They thought because he was old and infirm he should be an exception to the rule of women and children first. He vehemently refused to take the seat and didn't want special treatment. Mrs. Straus refused a seat because she didn't want to be separated from her husband of 40 years. They took their seats on the boat deck awaiting their death. Forty thousand New Yorkers attended the Memorial Service for the Straus's and people can still visit a little park at Broadway on 107th Street dedicated to their memory. The little park was once part of Isidor Straus's dairy farm.

If the Straus's were heroes, the tale of Sir Duff-Gordon and his wife Lucy was less than heroic. At the British enquiry into the TITANIC disaster Fireman Charles Hendrickson testified of his experiences in Number 1 Emergency Boat, a somewhat smaller boat than the rest of the life boats. Hendrickson testified that the boat had room for at least a dozen more people. It drifted about 200 yards from the ship. Hendrickson wanted to go back to look for survivors. "They would not listen to me", he testified. "Who was it who objected?", he was asked. "I think it was the women", he said. There were only two women in the boat; Lady Duff-Gordon and her Secretary. He was then closely questioned by the counsel representing the third class passengers. He had said that the coxswain had not paid any attention to his proposal to go back.

Q. You say that the attitude of his (the coxswain's) was due to the protests of the Duff-Gordons?

A. *Yes.*

Q. You say you heard cries?

A. *Yes.*

Q. Agonising cries?

A. *Yes, terrible cries.*

Q. At what distance?

A. *About 200 yards.*

Hendrickson later stated that the original objection to going back had been made by Lady Duff-Gordon and her husband had backed her up. Duff-Gordon himself then gave Hendrickson a cigar and gave all the members of the crew on the lifeboat "an order for five pounds". The Duff-Gordons, though, were not the only ones not to go back. The following is a verbatim exchange between Third Officer Pitman and Senator Smith before a Senate Committee of Enquiry in Washington D.C. nine days after the disaster. Pitman was in charge of Lifeboat No. 5.

Q. Officer, you really turned this No. 5 boat around to go in the direction from which these cries came?

A. *I did.*

Q. And were you dissuaded from your purpose by your crew?

A. *No, not crew; passengers.*

Q. One moment; by your crew and by the passengers in your boat?

A. *Certainly.*

Q. Then did you turn the boat towards the sea again?

A. *No, just simply took our oars in and lay quiet.*

Q. You mean you drifted?

A. *We may have gone a little bit.*

Q. Drifted on your oars?

A. *We may have drifted along. We just simply lay there doing nothing.*

Q. How many of these cries were there? Was it a chorus or was it - ?".

A. *I would rather you did not speak about that.*

Q. I would like to know how you were impressed by it.

A. *Well, I can not very well describe it. I would rather you would not speak of it.*

Q. I realise that this is not a pleasant theme, and yet I would like to know whether these cries were general and in chorus, or desultory and occasional?

A. *There was a continual moan for about an hour.*

Q. And you lay in the vicinity of that scene for about an hour?

A. *Oh, yes; we were in the vicinity of the wreck the whole time.*

Q. And drifted or lay on your oars during that time?

A. *We drifted towards daylight, as a little breeze sprang up.*

Q. Did this anguish or these cries of distress die away?

A. *Yes; they died away gradually.*

Q. Did they continue most of the hour?

A. *Oh, yes; I think so. It may have been a shorter time. Of course I did not watch every five minutes -*

Q. I understand that and I am not trying to ask about a question of five minutes. Is that all you care to say?

A. *I would rather that you would have left that out altogether.*

Q. I know you would; but I must know what efforts you made to save the lives of passengers and crew under your charge. If that is all the effort you made, say so - .

A. *That is all, Sir.*

Q. And I will stop that branch of my questioning.

A. *That is all, Sir, that is all the effort I made.*

Many maritime lessons were learnt from the tragedy. New laws were passed. Lifeboats must now be provided for all. Ships approaching ice must slow down or alter course. Rockets were offically recognised as international distress signals and banned for any other purpose. The United States was to expand its ice patrol which was to be financed by thirteen nations and is still active today. Regulations regarding wireless operations were also introduced.

It is, though, the haunting nature of one incident in the whole episode which shows how one tiny decision affected so many. It concerns the lookout, Fred Fleet. Of all who partook in the TITANIC tragedy, of all the people who later commented upon it or of all the people who wrote about it, or sat on enquiries over it, surely Fred Fleet must rank as the most important man in the entire story. He was the lookout who saw the iceberg.

In the second class saloon, Rev. Carter, who had been conducting hymn singing, received a final request about 10 o'clock. It was for the hymn, entitled, "For Those In Peril On The Sea". "In this ship", he said, "we are not in peril; but others may be. Let us sing the hymn for them". Even clergymen can presume too much. One and a half hours later the TI-TANIC and all those on board were in extreme peril.

The TITANIC carried six specialist outlooks, more than other ship in the world. They were two hours on and four hours off in the crow's nest reached by a ladder inside the forward mast, 98 feet above the water line. The crow's nest was equipped with a bell to which a rope pull was attached, a telephone on the starboard side connected with the bridge and behind the two lookouts were two canvas screens to shut out the light from aft.

George Hogg and Alfred Evans had been on duty from 6 p.m.- 8 p.m.; George Symons and Archie Dual from 8 p.m.- 10 p.m.; Fred Fleet and Reggie Lee came on at 10 o'clock. They received orders to keep a sharp lookout for ice. Fred Fleet took the port side and Lee the starboard. Fred was an orphan. His mother had left when he was a baby and he was brought up in one of Dr. Barnardo's homes until he was twelve. He then went to a training ship until he was sixteen and started out as a deck boy. He moved on to become an Able Seaman. When he climbed the lookout ladder on the TITANIC at 10 p.m. on April 14th, 1912, he was 24 years of age.

Just after seven bells (11.30 p.m.) Fred saw "a black mass" right ahead of the TITANIC. "It was the beautifullest night I ever seen", Fred told the author Leslie Reade 50 years later. "The stars were like lamps. I saw this black thing looming up; I didn't know what it was. I asked Lee if he knew what it was. He couldn't say. I thought I had better ring the bell. I rang it three times". He then went straight to the telephone and rang the bridge and cried, "Iceberg straight ahead!".

First Officer William Murdoch was in charge on the bridge and immediately ordered that the massive vessel be put "hard-a-starboard", meaning, under the system of helm orders then in force, that the ship's head would to go port. Then Murdoch ordered, "Stop. Full speed astern". He then pulled the switch that closed the water tight doors in the boiler and engine rooms. It was Murdoch's purpose that first having put the TITANIC to port, he would then turn her again to starboard to get around the iceberg. But it was all in vain. The iceberg was too close. When it struck the TITANIC was still turning to port and the spurs of the iceberg cut, foot after foot, a 300 foot, non-continuous gash beginning about 20 feet aft of her bows in the starboard side of her hull below the water line. Her first five forward water tight compartments were ruined and the great ship was doomed.

The incredible fact that emerged from the subsequent enquiries into the tragedy was that Fred Fleet, and the other lookouts, had not been supplied with binoculars. George Hogg later testified, "I have always had glasses and I did not see why I should not have them. I had them from Belfast to Southampton but from Southampton to where the accident occurred we never had them I asked for the glasses several times".

Why was the lookout locker empty of binoculars? Where had they gone? What we do know is that Symons had reported their disappearance to the Second Officer, Herbert Lightoller in Southampton and Lightoller said that he had passed on the message to the First Officer, Murdoch. In all of the hustle and bustle and changing of duties at Southampton the binoculars had been overlooked. The Chain of Command, somewhere along the line, had broken down and the detail did not seem significant at the time. All of the lookouts were resentful that they were deprived of the most vital tool of their trade. Fred Fleet maintained to the day of his death that if he had had binoculars he could have seen the iceberg earlier and the ship could have been saved. Indeed if he had seen it even a few seconds earlier Murdoch's evasive action might have been effective and the iceberg would have slipped by.

Fred Fleet's answers at the British Enquiry make for very chilling reading. When asked that if, with glasses, he would have seen the iceberg sooner, he replied, "Certainly".

Q. How much sooner do you think you would have seen it?
A. *In time for the ship to get out of the way.*
Q. So that is your view that if you had had glasses it would have made all the difference between safety and disaster?
A. *Yes.*
Q. After all, you are the man who discovered the iceberg?
A. *Yes.*
Q. Would you have used them constantly?
A. *Yes.*

In later years little did the people who bought the "SOUTHAMPTON EVENING ECHO" from the man at the corner of Market Street realise that the seller was the lookout who first saw the iceberg that sank the TITANIC. The memory of the slow advance of that "black thing" haunted him for many years after the wreck. Eventually he went to a doctor for help but sadly, on Janaury 11th 1965, Fred Fleet committed suicide in Southampton. It is a mind bending fact that the whole tragedy of the TITANIC could have been avoided if Fred Fleet and his associates had been given binoculars. On the decision not to concentrate on this detail hung the lives of 2,227 passengers and it subsequently cost the lives of 1,522 of them.

One thing is for sure, it certainly pays to, as the Americans put it, "sweat the small stuff" in life. No matter how big, gigantic, fantastic, innovative or wonderful, new technology may be, attention to every day detail in life, matters. When Dr. Robert D. Ballard discovered the haunting wreck of the legendary lost liner on September 1st, 1985, some of the most moving pictures to emerge from her grave two and a half miles down was of the telephone still hanging on the crow's nest that was Fred Fleet's lookout post. No doubt the locker is still empty of binoculars.

The Wandering Microbe

The decision by Sir Alexander Fleming to investigate an unusual happening that led to possibly the most momentous discovery in the history of medicine.

AYRSHIRE IS SET ON THE SOUTHERN UPLANDS OF SCOTLAND. ITS FERTILE COASTAL PLANE IS FAMOUS FOR THE JEWEL THAT IS TURNBERRY GOLF COURSE.

A journey from beautiful and turreted Culzean Castle near Turnberry soon brings the traveller through the pleasant seaside towns of Ayr and Troon and on to Largs, all the time looking across to Arran and the majestic Mull of Kintyre. It is a place of woods and rivers and fertile farms and canny, cautious people famous for a sense of pauky humour put across with a very straight face.

Ayrshire people, though, are not beyond romance, by any means, and are proud of their most famous son, the poet, Robert Burns. Coming a very close second in popular acclaim comes the son of an Ayrshire hill farmer called Hugh Fleming and his wife Grace. They farmed 800 acres at Loughfield about four miles from Darvel, a little lace-making town on a reach of the Upper Irvine River. Their third child was called Alexander, or Alec, as he was affectionately known.

Remembered by one of his teachers as "a dear little boy with dreamy blue eyes, Alec first went to school when he was five. It was a tiny little schoolhouse built on Loudon Moor, about a mile from Loughfield by the Glen Water. It had a single classroom for ten children taught by Lizzie Harrow, a young teacher in her twenties. Lizzie was not averse to taking her class down to the river after lunch to continue their education in the open air. She was a serious and efficient teacher.

We are told that when a school inspector was seen approaching in his trap, from a long way off, Lizzie and her pupils would hurry back to the classroom by a shortcut, entered by a window at the back. They were all in their places looking very serious indeed, if not slightly breathless, by the time the inspector arrived!

Alec lived with his sister Grace and brothers John and Robert in a farm-house where paraffin lamps lit the kitchen and candles lit the bed-rooms. There was no piped water, no bathroom, and certainly no indoor sanitation. The family washed in the kitchen sink in water drawn in buckets from the spring above the house. They were well clothed and there was plenty of good, fresh food. Often in winter there were very severe snow-storms and Alec would later recount how his mother sometimes gave her children two piping hot potatoes to keep their hands warm during their walk to school. "I think," said Alec in later years, "I was fortunate in being brought up as a member of a large family on a remote farm. We had no money to spend, and there was nothing to spend money on. We had to make our own amusements, but that is easy in such surroundings. We had the farm animals and the trout in the burn. We unconsciously learnt a great deal about nature, much of which is missed by a town-dweller." The children learned to look after themselves and became tough and confident. Alec and Robert knew every bird by name and the movements of the migrants. Swallows and clovers, curlews, larks and meadow-pipits, moss-cheepers and thrushes sang all around them. Wild duck and gulls, herons and snipe, sandpipers and hawks frequented the skies above them.

One thing left an impression upon Alec which was never to be re-moved. At the age of 10 he left the Loudon Moor school for a larger one at Darvel and one day he happened to run round the corner of a wall and collided with a boy named Jackson who was smaller than he was. The cartilage on his nose was broken and the change in his looks was obvious. Yet, since he suffered no more pain, it was not thought necessary to send him to see a doctor. So it was that Alexander Fleming had a boxer's nose for the rest of his life!

At the age of 12 he was sent to Kilmarnock Academy where he was ahead of his contemporaries by at least a year. He had very quick intelligence, a first class memory and though he did not talk much was very observant and critical.

He only stayed at the Academy for eighteen months when it was decided by his widowed mother and his elder brother, Hugh, who ran the farm, that he should accept an offer to go and live in London with his brother Tom who was a doctor. Six months later his brother Robert joined him and the young Scot started out in a new life which was to have incredible repercussions for mankind.

Alec, now 16, took a job in Leadenhall Street as a junior clerk in the America Line. It was a first class company and he was paid ten shillings a week but he soon found it to be a boring job. He followed the strict dress code of clerks in those days, wearing a straw hat in summer and bowler in winter with tweed jackets and trousers and high starched collars.

There was latitude in the use of ties and Alec always wore a bow tie. It was to be his "trade mark" for the rest of his life.

At the suggestion of his brother Tom, Alec decided to become a medical student. It was, as far as the medical world is now concerned, a decision which would lead to the worldwide transformation of the treatment of infectious diseases. It was, however, a decision that does not seem to have been made for any great altruistic reasons. Alec became a doctor to escape boredom! He took to medicine with a vengeance, even though he was two to three years older than most first year medical students. He didn't have any qualifications for entering a medical school so he found a teacher who coached him in the evenings. He gained top place in a very tough open examination which qualified him for entrance to medical school. He decided to enter St. Mary's Hospital Medical School and always said he went there because he had played a water polo match against their team. From such tiny incidents do great events come: Alexander Fleming was to spend his entire working life at St. Mary's, exactly 51 years in total!

Alec collected a lot of scholastic prizes on his way to qualification as a doctor in 1906, passing his exams with ease. It has been said that he had a real flair for working out what an examiner wanted and an ability to give them what they wanted with brevity and clarity. In the summer of 1906 Fleming joined the staff of Sir Almoth Wright at St. Mary's and stayed in it for 49 years! As a pathologist with deep interest in bacteriology, Wright had become head of both departments at St. Mary's in 1908.

It was a place of tremendous intellectual activity and research. Sir Almoth could speak seven languages, read eleven and could quote 20,000 lines of poetry! Deep and wide ranging were the discussions at teatime every day when Wright "took the chair". "Little Flem", as he became known, soon became a very popular member of Sir Almoth's staff and one of his most ardent disciples. The big interest of the department was their research on the immunity conferred by vaccination. Sir Almoth was convinced that the effective treatment for bacterial disease lay in the natural defences of the body against bacteria and their artifical stimulation. The inoculation department at St. Mary's was busy under Wright's team and the wards of the hospital full as patients came for vaccine therapy.

In 1908 Fleming actually qualified as a surgeon but decided to stay with Sir Almoth having now become deeply enthused by the whole world of pioneering in a laboratory. Few and far between were the laboratory workers who were fully qualified surgeons.

On the 28th June 1914 the heir to the Austrain throne, the Arch Duke Francis Ferdinand was assassinated. The event triggered Western Europe into the tragic first World War. Immediately Almoth Wright placed his whole department at the disposal of the Government for the production of vaccines. As it turned out, Wright and his staff were posted to Bologne in uniform to particularly study the surgical treatment of infected wounds. They were attached to a British Army General Hospital which was housed in the Casino. The conditions were frighteningly filthy around row upon row of camp beds on which lay the wounded of the Marne, Mons and Ypress.

On the top floor of the Casino Sir Almoth Wright established a laboratory which Fleming came to regard as the best he had ever worked in. It was, though, his own ingenuity that created the laboratory. There was no water, gas or drainage but we are told that Fleming contrived "incubators heated by paraffin stoves, bunsen burners running on alcohol, glass-blowing burners using fire bellows and a system of petrol cans and pumps to supply water."

In Bologne Fleming took swabs from wounds before, during and after surgery and surrounded by the sad and desperate conditions of the dead and dying made a very intensive study of the bacteriology of wound infection. He wrote two papers on his findings in "The Lancet" in 1915. It was a frustrating time with medical opinion divided over the use of antiseptics and the lack of success in protecting the wounded from gas-gangrene. Fleming commented that "surrounded by all those infected wounds, by men who were suffering and dying without being able to help them, I was consumed by a desire to discover, after all the struggling and waiting, something which would kill those microbes". In 1919 Lt. Col. Fleming was demobilised.

In December 1915 Fleming, while on leave, had married a nurse called Sarah McElroy from Ballina in Co. Mayo. Together they bought a beautiful country home in Suffolk with "a gravel drive lined by shrubs and an attractive glazed front door flanked by stone seats". It came with a fair amount of land and a stretch of river where there was good fishing. With enthusiasm Dr. and Mrs. Fleming transformed the meadow orchard around the house into a well designed garden. They had a large kitchen garden, two greenhouses, a vine and peaches trained against the wall. On the river bank they built a boat house in which they kept a punt. They called their home "The Dhoon".

The Flemings lived in London during the week and went to "The Dhoon" at weekends and at holidays. Alec, of course, returned to the

Innoculation Department at St. Mary's Hospital. In 1924 Sarah gave birth to a son, Robert, and in 1928 Alec became a Professor, being given the Chair of Bacteriology at the Medical School at St.Mary's. In all history there has never been a more famous medical Professor and September 1928 was to become etched in medical history as a truly momentous month.

Professor Fleming had, for a very long time, been hunting for a substance which would kill pathogenic microbes without damaging the patient's cells. One September morning in 1928 that substance floated in through the window or the ever open door of his laboratory at St. Mary's and landed on his bench. It was an unknown visitor.

Fleming had been studying a bacteria called Staphylococci and had been growing colonies of the bacteria, activated on agar in Petri dishes. There were a lot of these dishes cluttered on a disorderly way on Fleming's bench. The disorder, though, was about to produce a stupendous result. The lid had to be taken off Fleming's Petri dishes for the contents to be exposed under the microscope and they often got contaminated with mould from microbes that fell out of the air. On that September morning, though, a wandering micro-organism came into Fleming's laboratory which was to change all our lives.

Fleming was chatting to a colleague and while speaking he lifted some old Petri dishes and removed the lids. Several of them had been contaminated by mould. Suddenly Fleming stopped talking and after studying the mould in one particular dish for a minute he said, "That's funny ....." " He noticed that all around the mould the colonies of Staphylococci had been dissolved and instead of forming opaque yellow masses, they looked like drops of dew.

Professor Fleming decided to immediately take action. His colleague, Dr. D. M. Pryce, a Research Scholar at the time, later made a very significant comment about that morning. "What struck me was that he didn't confine himself to observing, but took action at once. Lots of people observe a phenomenon, feeling that it may be important, but, they don't get beyond being surprised - after which they forget. That was never the case with Fleming."

Immediately Fleming abandoned his investigation of the Staphylococci and gave himself to studying the mould. To his intense joy, after much observation, he had found the antibiotic of his dreams. He had discovered penicillin and had made, arguably, the most momentous discovery in medicine.

"Never neglect any appearance or any happening which seems to be out of the ordinary", said Fleming, later, "More often than not it is a false alarm, but it may be an important truth". It was that decision not to neglect the unusual that was to affect the treatment of infectious diseases forever.

Was it chance that brought that microbe floating into Fleming's laboratory? Was it coincidence that brought those two deep blue eyes to notice that a Petri dish was covered with recognisable colonies of Staphylococci except in the vicinity of a growth of mould near the edge of the dish? "All the same," said Fleming, "the spores didn't just stand up on the agar and say, "I produce an antibiotic, you know"". Indeed they didn't. The incredible story that unfolded that September morning in 1928 in London could perhaps be best summed up in the lines of the poet Kipling who wrote, "God took care to hide that country, till He judged his people ready. Then He chose me for His whisper, and I found it, and it's yours".

It took fifteen years for the full historical implications of what Fleming had discovered to become apparent. It came through the brilliant work of an Oxford team under the direction of Professor (later Lord) Florey and Dr. (later Sir) Ernest Chane, a young Jewish refugee from Hitler's regime. These men and their team gave pure penicillin to the world. Chane asked Fleming to send him a culture of penicillin, which he gladly did. With much labour and ingenuity the Oxford team overcame enormous difficulties and with undeviating dedication and numerous experiments, they proved the enormous therapeutic value of penicillin to the world. The romantic nature of Fleming's discovery has tended to overshadow the vital work of Florey and Chane but it must never be forgotten. It was more than appropriate that when the Nobel Prize for Medicine was announced in October 1945, it was to be awarded with equal division between Fleming, Florey and Chane.

The Oxford team collaborated with the Radcliffe Infirmary and in June 1941 it was given intravenously to a 14 year old boy with septicaemia. When the result was a complete cure, doctors started to use the word, "miracle". In the same month a 6 month old baby with Staphylococal infection of the urinary tract was given penicillin by mouth and was completely cured. In 87 out of 89 cases of eye infection where penicillin was administered under the direction of the Oxford team, a complete cure followed. Fifty cases of septic fingers, hands and wounds were healed locally by penicillin with tremendously rapid results.

In August 1942 Fleming re-entered the field of penicillin again. He had a patient from his brother's optical firm who had been admitted to St. Mary's with signs of meningitis. The patient seemed to be dying and no organisms had been found to account for his condition. Fleming was recalled from his holiday and succeeded in isolating the offending organism which he found to be sensitive to penicillin. He had no therapeutic penicillin. He appealed to Florey in Oxford by telephone to send him some quickly. It is reckoned that Florey took the penicillin by train from Oxford to Paddington himself and explained to Fleming how to use it. For seven days Fleming gave the patient injections but when the signs of brain infection continued, he telephoned Florey suggesting that the penicillin should be injected intrathecally. Penicillin had never been given by this route to a human being so Florey said he would try it on an animal. Fleming, however, with great courage decided he could not wait for the results of the experiment and gave his patient an intrathecal injection of penicillin followed by four similar injections during the next seven days. There was, almost immediately, a very dramatic improvement. The patient's symptoms disappeared and he walked out of hospital completely cured in a few weeks.

As it happened, the animal that Florey injected died an hour or two afterwards and if Fleming had known the result of this experiment, he may never have given his patient the life-saving intrathecal injection of penicillin.

Penicillin now found its way across the world and by May 1943 the United States Army put an order in for 20 million units. Incredible fame began to lay hold on the shy, quiet, Scot. He was elected a Fellow of the Royal Society, the highest honour which could be given him by his peers. In July 1944 he was awarded a Knighthood in the New Honours List. He was awarded the Freedom of Paddington and in 1946 of Darvel in Ayrshire. He was given an honorary doctorate by Harvard and Princeton Universities in the United States. He was also given honoray doctorates by the Universities of Durham, Paris, Louvin, Rome, Liege, Dublin, Athens, Belfast, St. Andrews, London, Bristol, Salonika, Edinburgh, Sao Paulo, Bordeaux and Vienna. He was made an honorary member of the Kiowa Tribe (Maker of Great Medicine). He was made a Commander of the Legion of Honour in France and was made Lord Rector of Edinburgh University. His phone rang from morning to night. Journalists from all over the world wanted to talk to him. He travelled the world as a hero and even had a crater on the moon named after him.

Pneumonia, syphilis, scarlet fever, boils, abscesses, both internal and external and almost any infection known to mankind fled from the penicillin he discovered.

After his death on March 11th, 1955 his ashes were interred in the crypt of St. Paul's Cathedral at a special ceremony. Enormous crowds had gathered outside the Cathedral and a very large congregation inside. Sir Alexander Fleming's friend of over 50 years, Professor C. A. Pannett rose to pay tribute. He said that his friend had "saved more lives and relieved more suffering than any other living man, perhaps more than any man who has ever lived". "We can", he said, "almost see the finger of God pointed to the direction his career should take at every turn". That finger certainly guided those blue eyes to the effects of the wandering microbe on that momentous September morning and the practice of medicine has never been the same since.

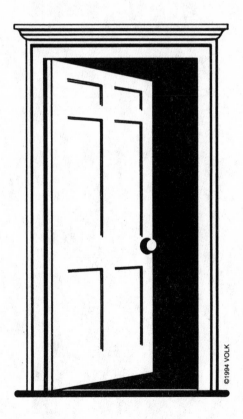

Dislike Of The Unlike

**Hitler's decision to exterminate
European Jews.**

LORD JAKOBOVITS, THE ONLY CHIEF RABBI OF THE UNITED KINGDOM EVER TO BE ELEVATED TO THE HOUSE OF LORDS APPEARED ONE EVENING ON B.B.C. TELEVISION AND HIS INTERVIEWER ASKED HIM WHY HE THOUGHT JEWS HAD BEEN SO SEVERELY PERSECUTED DOWN THROUGH THE CENTURIES. "IT IS DISLIKE OF THE UNLIKE", HE SAID.

Martin Luther certainly disliked Jews. When he was asked advice in 1543 as to how they should be treated he said, "First their synagogues should be set on fire and whatever does not burn should be covered or spread over with dirt so that no-one may ever be able to see a cinder or stone of it". He urged that Jewish homes should be "broken down or destroyed". He further urged that Jews should be put to work to earn their living "by the sweat of their noses", or, if regarded even then as too dangerous, these "poisonous bitter worms" should be stripped of their belongings "which they have extorted usuriously from us" and driven out of the country "for all time". ("On Jews and Their Lies", Wittenburg 1543).

Anti-Semitism has long been a feature in world history. It was present when 2 million of the children of Abraham faced genocide under an Egyptian Pharoah. It was present when the Assyrians took them into exile in Babylon. Alexander the Great was very fair to the Jews when he conquered Palestine in 332 B.C. but when they were conquered by Antichus of Syria he treated them barbarously. The Maccabees revolted and won independence again only to find it taken away by the Romans who were harsh and cruel. When the Jews rebelled the Roman's reprisal was to destroy Jerusalem in A.D. 70. This led to the Jewish dispersion throughout Europe. They settled in places as far apart as Babylon, North Africa and Spain where they greatly enriched life. In the 15th century they began to face expulsion.

In England where they had arrived with the forces of William the Conqueror as traders, they were later expelled in 1290 by Edward I only returning, under Cromwell, in the middle of the 17th century. Across Europe Jewish fortune varied and they were murdered in thousands in Germany by the Crusaders on their way to Palestine. In Italy Jews were confined in special parts of towns, namely the Ghetto. In Eastern Europe, during the 19th century, Jews were persecuted without mercy under Russian rulers and tens of thousands were massacred. Nearly one million left Russia for Western Europe or the United States. A Zionist movement began to stir in the early 19th century when Jews all over the world began to think of returning to Palestine. The 1917 British Government Balfour Declaration promised to set up a national home for the Jews in Palestine.

Few decades have passed in the last 2000 years in European history without Jews being accused of murdering christian children in order to use their blood in the baking of the Passover bread. This totally unjustified prejudice refuses to go away, despite education, and hatred of Jewish people has constantly been used as a fanned instrument of scapegoat politics. Before the promise of the Balfour Declaration could take place, a new threat arose as no other in history. It was in the form of the son of an Austrian customs official called Adolf Hitler who wanted to study art but who had failed the entrance exam to the Academy of Fine Arts in Vienna. No human being, so far in history, has been guilty of such cruelty to the Jewish people. Hitler, was, in the end, to lead a tacit, unrecorded connivance of thousands of people, including administrators and bureacrats, who would co-ordinate the systematic murder of at least six million Jewish men, women and little children. It was the most horrible of all horrors, it was the Holocaust. The blood of its victims still cries from the ground.

When in 1933 President Hindinburgh called on Hitler to form a government of "national concentration", representatives from the Conservative right reckoned they could keep him on a tight rein. They were to pay dearly for this illusion. In a few months he had silenced any support for them that might have threatened him. He then brought about the disillusion of all political organisations and his Nazi party emerged as the sole force in political power. Hitler and his Nazi regime set themselves to indoctrinate the German people with their vision of the world. It was a terrifyingly anti-Jewish vision.

To understand the background to the Nazi regimes diabolical decision to exterminate every European Jew, it is necessary to understand Hitler's thinking on the subject. He, in the end, must bear responsibility for instigating it. Right from his days in the German Army in the First World War, in which he was gassed and wounded, he was a fanatical anti-Semite. He blamed Germany's collapse on the weakness of an Imperial Government and the Jewish people. He believed Jews were bound by a plot to dominate the world and that their every activity was geared to this end. He believed them to be a parasitic race, exploiting labour and destructive by nature and incapable of establishing their own state.

Hitler believed the Jews would stoop to anything to reach their goal. He reckoned they had two major approaches to achieve what they were after. The first was to internationalise economics by financial gain to bring them under Jewish control. The second was to divide people against each other by Marxist agitation and doom them to civil wars that destroyed their powers of resistance. He was certain they were the enemies of any real national independence.

His was not an original view, of course. He was the direct heir of theories that had been circulating in Europe for decades. This view ignored Jewish history which shows Jewish people enormously enriching the life of nations to which they have been scattered (the "Dispora"). It ignored the many famous Jewish poets, philosophers, musicians, writers, scientists and teachers who contributed immensely to the quality of life that Europe enjoyed. It also ignored the indisputable fact that far from being a group bonded by a desire for world domination, the Jewish people have many conflicting movements within their own movement.

Hitler, of course, used the Jewish people, as had many others before him, as a scapegoat for national problems. It was an unbelievably unfair logic that identified Jews as being the evil principle that explained the calamities of the times. Hitler's view was devastatingly evil. In 1939, as World War II began, Albert Camus wrote in his notebook, "The reign of beasts has begun". Evil works by dehumanising that which opposes its view. It has a perverse efficient logic; identifying others as evil justifies all further evil against them. A person, for example, will kill a snake without any grief. This is because a snake is considered an evil thing with evil designs and is a different order of being. So Hitler's vocabulary in his speeches implied such an attitude to the Jews, he called them microbes, parasites,leeches, spiders - repulsive vermin whose extermination brings relief. Hitler believed in a social Darwinism where a natural aristocracy emerged. The Aryan race, a Nordic non-Jewish type, of supposed Indo-European descent, were the apex of the pyramid and other European peoples about the middle.

One of the techniques of evil is to get people to think in categories. In modern history Hitler had not been the only master of such a technique. Leninist zealots thought nothing of seeking to exterminate the "bourgeoise". Chairman Mao's zealots sought to exterminate China's intellectual class.

Pol Pot's Khmer Rouge murdered tens of thousands who spoke French, wore glasses or had soft hands. Evil is merciless and relentless and Hitler was very evil.

It is hard to believe he was a human being at all. Yet, he was. He had a sense of humour. He had excessive good manners to visitors. He even had an infantile side in loving the cowboy and Indian stories of Karl May. In childhood he showed little sign of abnormality and he could never have risen to power on anti-Semitism alone. He took a nation in decline and eight years later she was the mistress in Europe. He was not a frenzied hysteric devoid of self-control nor did he constantly rant and rave at his subordinates. When Hitler was at Berchtesgaden he loved to see the neighbourhood children and give them ice cream and cake.

One of his great gifts was that he could simplify very complex problems and he could think consistently. The sickening and horrifying thing was that he used his gifts to evil ends because of twisted, ill-founded thinking. It reminds us all that it is not what we think we are, it is what we think - we are. It also reminds us that Hitler was not a demagogue who appeared from nowhere and that a repitition of similar developments could precede a similar outcome in our world in the future.

Hitler certainly believed he had been given the task of ridding the earth of what he saw as the Jewish peril. It was a question of national revival versus international Jewry and it is obvious from any close study of his life that if Germany were to suffer another defeat it would not occur except at unimaginable cost to the Jews. It was certainly made very clear that if any foreign army dared to enter Germany, it would have to make it across the corpses of Jews. The dislike of the unlike was, in Hitler's mind and in the minds of his followers, a ticking bomb.

Historians argue as to the process of Hitler's thinking regarding the extermination of the Jews and did homicidal potential become murderous intent? When, then, did murderous intent become an extermination plan? Some would argue that it would be wrong to infer that Hitler's unconditional objective was to exterminate the Jews but one thing is for sure, it unquestionably became just that. From 1933- 1939 he first embarked on translating his anti-Semitism into acts. A flood of measures were passed against the Jews. It began, in the early months, with Nazi stormtroopers savagely beating Jewish pedestrians, often taking their money from them. It then proceeded to local authorities firing their Jewish employees. A law was then passed excluding Jews from public office. World opinion immediately stirred against Germany and a boycott of

German goods was called for. Hitler believed that the boycott had been stirred by Jews abroad and reacted by declaring that German Jews would suffer the consequences of the boycott. He used them as hostages. Everything moved towards making their lives in Germany impossible.

By 1935 it became a restriction of access to public buildings and public places. Then marriages between Jews and Germans were banned. Jews were given the status of second class citizens. In 1938 the expulsion of Jews from the German economy became the order of the day. Soon the policy against them was to ensure, by compulsory emigration, their departure from Germany and their resettlement in distant territories. The emigration policy however had one frightening element which now emerged. In a speech before the Reichstag on the 30th January 1939, Hitler prophesied that if international Jewry, in and outside Europe, once again forced the nations into a world war, the result would not be the Bolshevization of the earth and victory for the Jews but the annihilation of the Jewish race in Europe.

The genesis of the Holocaust lay right there. He was saying that if a world war came, meaning that his plan was endangered, then European Jews would not be around to enjoy their victory. The prophesy in his speech was soon to become an all too horrific reality. The most profound catastrophe Western civilization ever permitted or endured now edged ever closer.

On August 18th, 1941 Geobells submitted the proposal that every Jew should wear an insignia and Hitler accepted it. On September 1st the public proclamation declared that all Jews over six years old must wear a hexagonal yellow star, known as the Star of David, with the word 'Jew' at the centre. It was to be sewn on to their clothing. It is important to note that the correct translation of "Magen David" from which the term comes, is "Shield of David", not "Star of David". The Nazis transmuted it from a symbol of honour to a badge of derision. It was meant to transform them from members of the community into strangers. It was no longer a shield of armour to defend and protect but an insignia of cloth which exposed and jeopardised.

Nazis would stop people on the street and ask them to take off their coat. If they didn't have a star on their jacket or shirt under their coat, they would have them prosecuted or punished or beaten or even shot. Even if one of the prongs was not properly sewn on it brought harrassment. As Jews passed the Nazis would yell at them, "Yid, dirty yid!". The star was feared for its consequences.

The plethora of laws, edicts and regulations now harrassed and morti-fied the Jewish population. Their movements in every facet of ordinary life was regulated. The children, for exmaple, could no longer, in effect, go to the park or the zoo or the ice cream parlour or the cinema, the museum or the library. They were restricted to their own homes, gardens and court yards.

September 1941 was not just the time for the Insignia Order, the end of the month brought another measure to seal the doom of the Jewish people; their deportation to the East was ordered. Their homes and gar-dens and courtyards were to be left behind. The saddest thing of all was that for most of them they were to be left behind for ever; Heydrich told Eichman that "the Fuhrer has ordered the physical destruction of the Jews". At his later trial in Jerusalem Eichman said on July 11th, 1961 that Heydrich "spoke that sentence to me. And as if he then wished to ob-serve the effect of his words, quite contrary to his custom, he paused for a long while. I can still remember it today." Six million Jews were soon to know the deadly impact of it.

The preparations for extermination were soon getting under way. The first trains began to roll on October 16th. On November 14th a series of trains departed for the Soviet Union for the German army had already stormed across the Soviet frontier overwhelming a poorly prepared enemy. Most of the passengers on the trains were shot upon arrival. In early December the local Jews were gassed to death at the little Polish town of Chelmno in a newly built death camp.

On January 20th, 1942 the infamous Wannsee Conference was held just outside Berlin. No mention was made about the fact that in the previous forty-four days more than forty thousand Jews and Gypsies had been murdered at Chelmno. Heidrich began the Conference by telling the assembled civil servants that he had been appointed "as Plenipotentiary for the preparation of the Final Solution of the European Jewish question". Up until now the struggle against the Jews had involved their expulsion from the living space of German people. Now the Conference was told that all this was "merely a measure of expediency in view of the approaching final solution of the Jewish question".

This solution, he explained, concerned not only those Jews under German rule but "some eleven million Jews" throughout Europe, including, he said, three hundred and thirty thousand in unconquered Britain, eighteen thousand in Switzerland, fifty-five thousand five hundred in European Turkey, ten thousand in Spain, eight thousand in Sweden, three thousand in Portugal, three hundred and forty-two thousand in Romania, fifty-eight thousand in Italy, forty thousand in Croatia, two thousand three hundred in Finland, four thousand in the Irish Republic etc. He did not mention that German death squads had already murdered two hundred thousand Jews of pre-war Lithuania between July and November 1941. Meticulously he spoke of the two million more Jews in the Ukraine and of those in Hungary, France, Morocco, Algeria, Tunisia, etc.

Long hours were spent discussing the deportation and destruction of millions of people. Was there ever, in history, a Conference quite like it? The plan was that whole Jewish communities would be uprooted step by step and disappear. The general feeling was that few would care to enquire what had become of them. As Martin Gilbert has stated, "What had hitherto been tentative, fragmentary and spasmodic was to become formal, comprehensive and efficient". The apparatus of total destruction was now perfected under the cover of a complex system of subterfuge. On the surface the whole system was called a "resettlement" of the Jews. It was in effect a resettlement to their graves. Hitler spoke in the Sports Palace in Berlin ten days after the Wannsee Conference stating that "the result of this war will be the complete annihilation of the Jews". His words, as far as Europe was concerned, very nearly came true.

As we look back upon it all the words Belzec, Treblinka, Auchwitz-Birkenau, Chelmno, Buchenwald, Belsen, and Sachesenhausen now strike a dull ache into late twentieth century hearts. The whole thing still weighs heavily on the European conscience. Even Steven Speilberg's "Schindler's List" cannot hope to ultimately convey the horror of it. In conversation with the author the Auchwitz survivor Helen Lewis greatly applauded Speilberg's faithful attempt to tell it like it was, but she commented that there was one difference between the film and her experiences at Auchwitz. It was that her experiences were worse.

How, in this short essay, can the immensity of the Nazi crime be fathomed? All who try to evaluate it are eventually paralysed. It is a bottomless pit. Even recent revelations about Hitler's bunker suicide in 1945 as the Soviet Army encircled Berlin brings no sense of justice for the blood that cries from the ground. The question, of course, arises that if only he had died in the August of 1941, would what followed have happened? The general feeling is that its impetus would have been lost. He had the last word and he was the prime mover that brought about the Holocaust.

How can words describe the result of Hitler's decision to exterminate every European Jew? Rudolph Reder, a soap manufacturer, and only one of two Jews to survive the Belzec concentration camp, has bravely tried. He was forced to work on the "death squads" at Belzec and his train was among the first to reach the death camp on August 11th, 1942, a month in which one hundred and forty-five thousand Jewish people were murdered at Belzec. That number represented less than half of the Jews murdered on the soil of German occupied Poland in that month alone. He wrote:

"About mid-day the train entered Belzec, a small station surrounded by small houses inhabited by the S.S. men. Here the train was shunted off the main track to a siding which ran about another kilometre straight to the gates of the death camp. Ukranian railway men also lived near the station and there was a post office nearby as well.

At Belzec Station an old German with a thick, black moustache climbed into the locomotive cab. I don't know his name, but I would recognise him again, he looked like a hangman; he took over command of the train and drove it into the camp. The journey to the camp took two minutes. For months I always saw the same bandit.

The siding ran through fields, on both sides there was completely open country; not one building. The German who drove the train into the camp climbed out of the locomotive, he was "helping us" by beating and shouting, throwing people out of the train. He personally entered each wagon and made sure that no-one remained behind. He knew about everything. When the train was empty and had been checked, he signalled with a small flag and took the train out of the camp.

The whole area of Belzec was occupied by the S.S. - no-one was allowed to approach; any individuals who stumbled accidentally into the area were immediately shot. The train entered a yard which measured about one kilometre by one kilometre and was surrounded by barbed wire and fencing, about two metres high, which was not electrified. Entry to the yard was through a wooden gate covered with barbed wire. Next to the gate there was a guard house with a telephone and standing in front of the guard house were several S.S. men with dogs. When the train had entered the yard the S.S. men closed the gate and went into the guard house.

At that moment dozens of S.S. men opened the doors of the wagons shouting "Los!". They pushed people out with their whips and rifles. The doors of the wagon were about one metre above the ground. The people, hurried along with blows from whips, were forced to jump down, old and young alike, it made no difference. They broke arms and legs, but they had to obey the orders of the S.S. men. Children were injured, everyone was falling down, dirty, hungry, frightened. Beside the S.S. men stood the so-called "Zugsfuhrers" - these were the guards in charge of the permanent Jewish death kommando in the camp, they were dressed in civilian clothes, without any insignia.

The old, the sick and the babies, all those who could not walk, were placed on stretchers and taken to the edge of the huge mass grave. There, the S.S. man Irrman shot them and then pushed them into the graves with his rifle. Irrman was the camp expert at "finishing off" old people and small children; a tall, dark, handsome Gestapo with a very normal-looking face, he lived like the other S.S. men in Belzec, not far from the railway station in a cottage, completely alone - and, like the others, without his family and without women.

He used to arrive at the camp early in the morning and meet the death transport. After the victims had been unloaded from the trains, they were gathered in the yard and surrounded by armed Ukranian S.S. men and then Irrman delivered a speech. The silence was deathly. He stood close to the crowd. Everyone wanted to hear, suddenly a feeling of hope came over them. "If they are going to talk to us, perhaps they are going to let us live after all. Perhaps we will have work, perhaps ... " Irrman spoke loudly and clearly, "Now you're going to the bath house, afterwards you will be sent to work". That's all. Everyone was happy, glad they were going to work. They even clapped.

I remember those words being repeated day after day, usually three times a day - repeated for the four months of my stay there. That was the one moment of hope and illusion. For a moment the people felt happy. There was complete calm. In that silence the crowd moved on, men strayed into a building on which there was a sign in big letters: "Bath and Inhalation Room".

The women went about twenty metres further on - to a large barrack hut which measured about thirty metres by fifteen metres. There they had their head shaved, both women and girls. They entered, not knowing what for. There was still silence and calm. Later I knew that only a few minutes after entering, they were asked to sit on wooden stools across the barrack hut, and Jewish barbers, like automations, as silent as the grave, came forward to shave their heads. Then they understood the whole truth, none of them could have any doubts any more.

All of them - everyone - except a few chosen craftsmen - were going to die. The girls with long hair went to be shaved. Those who had short hair went with the men - straight into the gas-chamber. Suddenly there were cries and tears, a lot of women had hysterics. Many of them went cold-bloodedly to their deaths, especially the young girls. There were thousands of intelligensia, many young men and - as in all other transports - many women. I was standing in the yard, together with a group left behind for digging graves, and was looking at my sisters, my brothers and friends being pushed to their death. At the moment when the women were pushed naked, shorn and beaten, like cattle to the slaughter, the men were already dying in the gas-chambers. The shaving of the women lasted about two hours, the same time as the murder process in the chamber.

Several S.S. men pushed the women with whips and bayonets to the building housing the chambers; three steps led up to the hall, and Ukranian S.S. men counted seven hundred and fifty people to each chamber. Those who did not want to enter were stabbed with bayonets and forced inside - there was blood everywhere.

I heard the doors being locked, the moaning, shouting and cries of despair in Polish and Jewish; the crying of the children and women which made the blood run cold in my veins. Then came one last terrible shout. All this lasted fifteen to twenty minutes after which there was silence. The Ukranian guards opened the doors on the outside of the building and I, together with the others, left over from the previous transports, began our work.

We pulled out the corpses of those who were alive only a short time ago, we pulled them using leather belts to the huge mass graves while the camp orchestra played; played from morning till night."

Reder was a member of the "Death Commando", consisting of five hundred able-bodied Jews, "selected" from the incoming transport. As he recounted it:

"The 'craftsmen' numbered two hundred and fifty but they did not do any work which required specialist knowledge - only digging the graves and dragging the corpses to them. We dug huge mass graves and dragged the bodies. We used spades, but there was also a mechanical excavator which dug up the sand and pulled it into mounds and later covered over the graves already full of bodies. About four hundred and fifty of us worked at the graves. It took a week to dig one pit. The most horrible thing for me was that there was an order to pile the bodies up to a level one metre above the edge of the graves and then cover with a layer of sand, while thick, black blood flowed out and flooded the ground like a lake. We had to walk along the ledges from one pit to the next, and our feet were soaked with our brothers' blood. We walked over their bodies and that was even worse.

The brute Schmidt was our guard; he beat and kicked us if he thought we were not working fast enough. He ordered his victims to lie down and gave them twenty-five lashes with a whip, ordering them to count out loud. If the victim made a mistake, he was given fifty lashes. No-one could withstand fifty lashes. Usually they managed somehow to reach the bar-rack-hut afterwards, but the following morning they were dead. This happened several times a week.

Thirty or forty of us were shot every day. A doctor usually prepared a daily list of the weakest men. During the lunch break they were taken to a nearby grave and shot. They were replaced the following morning by new arrivals from the first transport of the day. Our Kommando always numbered five hundred - we knew, for example, that although Jews had built the camp and installed the death engine, not one of them now re-mained alive. It was a miracle that anyone survived for five or six months in Belzec. When people who arrived on the transport begged for water, any of us who helped them were shot.

Besides digging graves, the death brigade had the task of dragging the bodies out of the chambers and piling them into a huge mound, after which they had to be dragged to the graves. The ground was sandy. One corpse was dragged by two men. We had leather belts which we tied around the wrists of the bodies. It often happened that the corpse's head dug into the sand while being dragged along. We carried the bodies of children, two at a time, one over each shoulder - this was a German or-der. We worked either at grave- digging or emptying the gas-chambers. We worked like this from early morning until night-fall. Only darkness halted our work."

Darkness, indeed. How often the point has been made that animals would not do what humans sometimes do? If proof were needed a trag-edy took place on September 1st, 1942 at Treblinka which proves that animals often behave better than humans. A Polish eyewitness to what went on was a railway man called Zabeki. He recalls that beyond the railway lines and parallel to them ran a concrete road beyond which was an excavation overgrown with bushes.

Sometimes as the trains arrived fugitives, seeing the thicket, would jump down from the trains and try to hide there. The S.S. men knew about this and scoured the thicket with a dog. Zabeki records that on September 1st he saw several people who had managed to break out of the trains making for the thicket. He writes:

"One of the S.S. men who had arrived at the station that day - he was Kurt Franz, Deputy Commandant of the Camp - came out with his dog along the road. The dog, scenting something, pulled the S.S. man after it into the thicket. A Jewess was lying there with a baby; probably she was dead. The baby, a few months old, was crying, nestling against its mother's bosom.

The dog, let off the lead, tracked them down, but at a certain distance it crouched on the ground. It looked as if it was getting ready to jump, to bite them and tear them to pieces. However, after a time it began to cringe and whimper dolefully, and approached the people lying on the ground; crouching, it licked the baby on its hands, face and head. The S.S. man came up to the scene with his gun in his hand. He sensed the dog's weakness. The dog began to wag its tail, turning its head towards the boots of the S.S. man.

The German swore violently and flogged the dog with his stick. The dog looked up and fled. Several times the German kicked the dead woman, and then began to kick the baby and trample on its head. Later, he walked through the bushes, whistling for his dog. The dog did not seem to hear, though it was not far away; it ran through the bushes whimpering softly; it appeared to be looking for the people.

After a time the S.S. man came out on to the road, and the dog ran up to its "master". The German then began to beat it mercilessly with a whip.

The dog howled, barked, even jumped up on the German's chest as if it were rabid, but the blows with the whip got the better of it. On the "master's" command it lay down.

The German went a few paces away, and ordered the dog to stand. The dog obeyed the order perfectly. It carefully licked the boots, undoubtedly spattered with the baby's blood, under its muzzle. Satisfied, the S.S. man began to shoot and set the dog on other Jews who were still escaping from the wagons standing in the station."

Obviously the animal did not naturally want to do what the German S.S. soldier did without demur. The tragedy of the Nazi regime was that by terror they even corrupted animals.

It is, at the time of writing, fifty years since the Soviet troops opened the gates of Auchwitz. As we look out across central Europe today, Hitler's prophesy of annihilating the Jewish people, fortunately did not take place. About two million Jews were left in Europe after the Nazi defeat, the very dim shadow of a once very vibrant community. Many of the traumatized survivors were repressed and secularised by more than four decades of communism. Yet all over Europe Judiasm is beginning to take root again. Jews are proudly calling themselves Jews once more and reviving traditions and cultures long buried in the ashes of Hitler's ovens or under the weight of Communist oppression. In Budapest, Prague, Warsaw, Moscow, Bratislava, Berlin, in hundreds of towns and villages from the Baltic to the Black Sea, Jews are once again returning to their ancient faith. One of the new phenomenas is that it is the younger Jews who are drawing their fathers back to the Jewish faith. Some young Germans with no Jewish background are even choosing to convert. Fortunately, Hitler did not in the end achieve his desire of making Germany free of Jews.

One thing is absolutely certain. If Hitler and his regime are not judged by God in a coming day for what they did to European Jews, Heaven will turn black. Another thing is also absolutely certain; Heaven will never turn black.

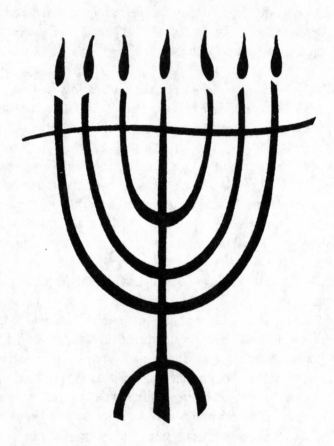

Two Hearts Beating Each To Each

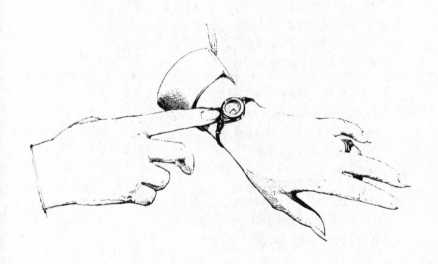

The decision of Elizabeth Barrett and Robert Browning that it was time to marry.

FEW WRITERS HAVE CAPTURED THE ESSENSE OF LOVE AND PASSION BETTER THAN ELIZABETH BARRETT BROWNING. IN MATTERS OF THE HEART SHE WAS A SUPERB OBSERVER.

Though afflicted with illness for the major part of her life and personal tragedy enough for many lives, when she lifted her pen to track love's course, her touch was sure, her gift, obvious. Take the following poem on the matter of how a woman's heart is permanently won.

THE LADY'S YES

"Yes", I answered you last night;
"No", this morning, sir, I say.
Colours seen by candle-light
Will not look the same by day.

When the viols played their best,
Lamps above and laughs below,
"Love me" sounded like a jest,
Fit for "Yes" or fit for "No".

Call me false or call me free -
Vow, whatever light may shine,
No man on your face shall see
Any grief or change on mine.

Yet the sin is on us both;
Time to dance is not to woo;
Wooing light makes fickle troth,
Scorn of me recoils on you.

Learn to win a lady's faith,
Nobly as the thing is high,
Bravely, as for life and death -
With a loyal gravity.

Lead her from the fest of boards,
Point her to the starry skies;
Guard her, by your truthful words,
Pure from courtships flatteries.

By your truth she shall be true,
Ever true, as wives of yore;
And her "Yes" once said to you,
SHALL be "Yes" for ever more.

What kind of man could win such a woman's heart? It is a question which has fascinated millions of lovers of English Literature (and lovers) for well over a century. From London's West End to Hollywood, various actors have tried to portray the life and personality of the man who loved Elizabeth Barrett.

To whom, then, did Elizabeth send the following letter post-marked Saturday evening, August 17th, 1846?

> " ... you were made perfectly to be loved - and surely I have loved you, in the idea of you, my whole life long. Did I tell you that before, so often as I have thought it? It is that which makes me take it all as visionary good - for when one's Ideal comes down to one, and walks beside one suddenly, what is it possible to do but cry out ...

> "A Dream"? You are the best ... best. And if you loved me only and altogether for pity, (and I think that, more than you think, the sentiment operated upon your generous chivalrous nature) and if you confessed it to me and proved it, and I knew it absolutely - what then?

> As long as it was love, should I accept it less gladly, do you imagine, because of the root? Should I think it less a gift?

Should I be less grateful, ... or more? Ah - I have my "theory of causation" about it all - but we need not dispute, and will not, on any such metaphysics. Your loving me is enough to satisfy me - and if you did it because I sat rather on a green chair than a yellow one, it would be enough still for me: - only it would not for you - because your motives are as worthy always as your acts. Dearest! ..... "

The object of the letter was, of course, one of the greatest poets of his age: Robert Browning. The sixteen years of his courtship and marriage to Elizabeth Barrett, are, in the annals of love, one of the most captivating in history. If Elizabeth could track love's course, what about Robert's superb tracking of love's anticipation in the following poem?

MEETING AT NIGHT

The grey sea and the long black land;
And the yellow half-moon large and low;
And the startled little waves that leap
In fiery ringlets from their sleep,
As I gain the cove with pushing prow,
And quench its speed in the slushy sand.

Then a mile of warm sea-scented beach,
Three fields to cross till a farm appears;
A tap at the pane, the quick sharp scratch
And blue spurt of a lighted match,
And a voice less loud, thro' its joys and fears,
Than the two hearts beating each to each!

What brought such gifted people together? The answer is, their poetry. Yet, interestingly, they also had something else in common in their background. Both their families were involved in slave sugar plantations in the West Indies.

Elizabeth's Barrett's great grandfather owned huge estates and tracts of land and hundreds of slaves in Jamaica. Sugar and rum were much in demand and were highly profitable. Edward Moulton- Barrett, Elizabeth's father, inherited property and slaves from his father. The slaves were eventually emancipated in 1833, and eventually Edward settled with his family in "Hope End" in Herefordshire in the Malvern Hills. The home was set in 475 acres which included picturesque woodland. He built an entirely new home in the Turkish style, fashionable at that time because of the Pavilion then being build by the Prince Regent. He was a hard working, high minded individual. He was by the standards of his time good to his family and deeply respected by them. His children more than welcomed him when he returned from his visits to London where he went on business connected with his Jamacian Estates.

Elizabeth was the eldest in a family of eight sons and three daughters and was born in 1806 at Coxhoe Hall, Northumberland. She was brought to her parent's new home at "Hope End" when she was three. She was the tomboy of the family and was full of high spirits. In her childhood she injured her spine while riding a pony and this kept her an invalid for several years. When she recovered she was able to walk perfectly well. Early in life she showed real literary talent and her father paid for a privately printed edition of her poem, "The Battle of Marathon" written when she was fourteen. She had a free run of her father's library and used it frequently. It was accepted by the Barrett children that their father knew best and that his will prevailed in their home. It was, as far as his family was concerned, the divine right of fathers. Little did Elizabeth dream that such blind obedience and love of another were to clash in one of the most famous love stories in history. Elizabeth was to be right at the centre of its drama for sixteen years. She was to become a very exceptional woman and one of the greatest poetesses in English literature. Eventually, of course, she was to break away in a spectacular way from her father's possessive control but it was quite some time before these events unfolded. Parental omnipotence ruled at "Hope's End". Even as a twenty-five year old at "Hope's End" Elizabeth did not leave the house without her father's permission. Eventually because of problems in business the Barretts had to move from "Hope's End" to Sidmouth in Devon, from 1832-1835. They eventually settled at 50 Wimpole Street in London.

Edward Moulton-Barrett was now without his estates in the West Indies and no longer held his high position in public life in Herefordshire. Socially he was no-one. His affectionate nature began to give way to the nature of a tyrant. Loss of "position" and the onset of boredom may have been the basis for the change in his nature, but, Elizabeth was to sadly find herself at its epicentre.

The cause of the clash was to come from a man whose family also had its roots in West Indian plantations. Robert Browning's grandparents had considerable wealth from plantations in the West Indian island of St. Kitts and his father was sent there to help administer them. He detested the system of slavery which he found on the family plantations and was so shocked and sickened by it, he decided to have nothing to do with it. He supported himself on the island and then returned to England to his father's utter astonishment and deep rage. As Robert Browning later remarked, "If we are poor it is to our father's infinite glory". He became an official in the Bank of England and lived comfortably in rural Camberwell. He built up a very fine library and read widely and his son called him "tenderhearted to a fault". His wife, Sarah, was a serene individual with a deep Christian faith and a love of music. They settled first at Southamptom Street, Camberwell with its fields and orchards and with the wooded Herne Hill and Dulwich hills surrounding them where they had a pageboy and servants in the home.

In 1840 the family moved to Hatcham, New Cross. Robert was fondly proud of his father's rebellion against slavery and held his mother, also, in deep affection. He never went to bed without giving her a goodnight kiss to the day he left home.

When Robert Browning decided that he wanted to become a poet his father backed him financially and to his last day on earth he was deeply grateful for this kindness. Robert believed that the financial facility given to him was a sacred trust. He said, as recorded in the "NEW YORK EVENING POST" in December 1889, "It would have been quite unpardonable in my case not to have done my best. My dear father put me in a condition most favourable for the best work I was capable of .... he secured for me all the ease and comfort that a literary man needs to do good work. It would have been shameful if I had not done my best to realise his expectations of me."

So it was that a room was set aside in the greener pastures of Hatcham for Robert to do his work. Its windows opened on to a view of chestnut trees, a holly hedge and to sheep bleating in nearby fields. Such a view was to influence Browning's later poem, "Home Thoughts From Abroad". When far from England he remembered the Browning garden at Hatcham:

"Oh, to be in England
Now that April's there
And whoever wakes in England
Sees some morning, unaware
That the lowest boughs and the brush-wood sheaf
Round the elm-tree bowl are in tiny leaf,
While the chaffinch sings on the orchard bough
In England - now!

And after April, when May follows,
And the white throat builds, and all the swallows -
Hark! where my blossomed pear-tree in the hedge
Leans to the field and scatters on the clover
Blossoms and dew drops - at the bent sprays edge,
That's the wise thrush; he sings each song twice over
Lest you think he never could recapture
That first fine careless rapture!

And though the fields look rough with hoary dew,
All will be gay when noontide wakes anew
The buttercups, the little children's dower -
Far brighter than this gaudy melon-flower!

In the early 1840's Browning was already beginning to rise as a poet and moved in very fashionable intellectual society. The great Thomas Carlyle commented of Robert that "among the men engaged in England in literature just now was one of the few from whom it was possible to expect something". He was not without his critics and failures but he showed deep confidence in what he believed to be a sacred trust put in him to be a poet of distinction. He was now thirty-four and "getting there". His poetry was being read, and unknown to him being read particularly by a poetess called Elizabeth Barrett.

Elizabeth, whose health declined in her twenties, was now actually suffering from tuberculosis. Sadly her brother Edward was drowned in a sailing tragedy in 1840 and Elizabeth's health, following the tragedy, had utterly collapsed. It was, in fact, five years before she could calmly reflect on the tragedy. She was put on drugs by her doctor and although never addicted to them she took them for the rest of her life.

Complete seclusion was considered by her medics as essential to her survival and she must stay, they said, in one room away from the danger of draughts. There, she put her books and paintings and busts of Chaucer and Homer and her engravings of Wordworth, Carlyle, Tennyson and Browning.

Despite her illness, Elizabeth had greatly matured in her writing and she who wrote a French heroic tragedy at the age of ten, and an imitated epic in four books at fourteen, had now had some of her work published in England and the United States in the early 1840's to considerable ac-claim. Sadly, though, her tuberculosis kept her very much a prisoner in her own home. Elizabeth did not go out and very few people visited her, though there were exceptions. Florence Nightingale actually walked round from Harley Street and delivered flowers to Elizabeth personally.

Her illness followed the pattern of tuberculosis which was a steady decline interrupted by temporary improvement. By the mid- 1840's Elizabeth was enjoying one of those periods of improvement though desperately impatient at her predicament. "Do you think I was born to live the life of an oyster such as I do live here?", she asked. "I still sit in my chair and walk about the room", she wrote as her health improved, "but the prison doors are shut close and I could dash myself against them sometimes with a passionate impatience of the needless captivity". At this period of time her constant spitting of blood had, thankfully stopped.

It was into such a sombre, depressing house set in the sooty air and fogs of central London that, one morning, love entered. It came in the form of a letter one winter's morning in January 1845. The sender had just returned to England from Italy late in the previous December to find that a friend of his, John Kenyon had sent his sister a copy of Elizabeth Browning's "Poems". In it he had found a poem entitled "Lady Geraldine's Courtship" and in the poem was a reference to his own work which had been entitled "Bells and Pomegranates". It stirred his heart, and, no wonder.

A page in the employ of Lady Geraldine reads to her a selectioon of other men's poetry:

" Or at times a modern volume - Wordsworth solemn-thoughted
idyl,
Howitt's ballad-verse, or Tennyson's enchanted reverie -
Or from Browning some 'Pomegranate', which, if cut deep
down the middle,
Shows a heart within blood - tinctured, of a veined
humanity!".

It is not recorded whether Browning blushed at such a line from a lady who was to be talked of, on the death of Wordsworth, as the next Poet Laureate. Blush or not, he talked to his friend John Kenyon about how to thank her. Kenyon, a published poet himself and a cousin and close friend of Elizabeth's advised him that his cousin was "a great invalid and sees no-one, but great souls jump at sympathy". He could have added that sympathy is often akin to love. Browning lifted his pen and wrote the letter that was to change his life and that began a love story which to this day affects millions by its pathos and drama. "I love your verses with all my heart, dear Miss Barrett", he wrote, " ... and I love you too".

By return of post on January 11th Robert received a letter from Elizabeth Barrett which showed how wise Kenyon's advice had been and how well he knew her. "Sympathy is dear - very dear to me", wrote Elizabeth, "but the sympathy of a poet, and such a poet, is the quintessence of sympathy to me".

Kenyon had offered to bring Browning to see Elizabeth back in 1841 but she had refused the offer. She had even refused to see Wordsworth because her illness was extremely debilitating and she shrank from meeting people she did not know well. Browning had hinted at his lost opportunity of meeting her in his first letter and Elizabeth now wrote, "Winters shut me up as they do dormouse's eyes; in the Spring we shall see: and I am so much better that I seem turning round to the outside world again".

So it was that letters had to be the bridge between their hearts for the next four months. They exchanged them several times a week. Who, when they feel the first stirrings of love does not have their doubts about where its increasingly overwhelming force is taking them? Elizabeth at first feared that Robert's love was only sympathy for her suffering. She soon found that his heart beat to more than the tune of sympathy, as Spring approached. "Dear warm Spring, dear Miss Barrett", wrote Robert, "And the birds know it; and in Spring I shall see you, - surely see you - for when did I once fail to get whatever I had set my heart upon?"

Love poems crossing the centuries from Solomon to Robert Burns, from Shakespeare to Thomas Hardy have been read by generations of people because they echo what has gone on in their own hearts. The poetic prose, though, that now flowed from the mind and hearts of Robert Browning to Elizabeth Barrett were exquisite. Browning wrote of "the octave on octaves of quite golden strings you enlarge the compass of my harp with". Elizabeth, in mid-April, admitted to Browning that she had written letters to him which she had never posted. If he knew of them she wrote, "you would not think for a moment that the east wind, with all the harm it does to me, is able to do the great harm of putting out the light of the thought of you to my mind".

Robert, early in March, suggested that he come to see Elizabeth but she put him off: "You are Paraelsus and I am recluse", she wrote. Love, though, always finds a way and on the 20th May she consented to seeing him, still allowing herself an escape route by offering Robert an excuse: "If you should not be well, pray do not come".

Robert Browning mounted the stairs of 50 Wimpole Street at exactly 3 p.m. on the Spring afternoon of May 20th, 1845. His eyes fell on a woman six years his elder. Elizabeth was handsome rather than pretty and her long hair fell around her face in the dark cork-screw ringlets which were fashionable at the time. Robert stayed for an hour and a half and told Elizabeth how he felt about her in his heart. She told him that if he ever discussed the subject again she would never see him again while she lived. How many a woman has said the same thing through history? She said it because she was unsure of the man with her at the time and was then filled with longing for him after he had gone.

But Robert in whose heart ran "arrowy fire, while earthly forms combine to throb the secret force" then wrote Elizabeth a letter putting down in writing his feelings for her. Her reply was swift: "Forget it once and forever, having said it at all .... now, if there should be one word of answer attempted to this: or of reference; I must not .... I will not see you again".

But the "arrowy fire" ran on and so did the letters and visits. Elizabeth tried another tact. She tried to plead that he was throwing his best affections into the ashes. She maintained that youth and cheerfulness were behind her but it all made no difference to Robert Browning. Soon Elizabeth saw very clearly that this man was in love with her. "A friend of mine", she wrote to a friend of hers outside of London, "one of the greatest poets in England - brought me primroses and polyanthuses the other day, as they are grown in Surrey". He brought her more than flowers, he brought her an improvement in her health and in her spirits for now she began to go down stairs and to occasionally go for drives in Regent's Park. She even went for drives as far as the Serpentine and Westminster Abbey and even to the slums of Shoreditch to buy back her spaniel Flush from dog-kidnappers!

But Elizabeth's feelings for her father were central in her developing relationship with Robert. "I might certainly tell you that my own father, if he knew that you had written to me so and that I had answered you - so, even, would not forgive me at the end of ten years .... for the singular reason that he never does tolerate in his family (sons or daughters) the development of one class of feelings," she wrote.

He was a very real threat to Robert Browning's love for Elizabeth. She was a woman of forty but was as powerless as a little child in how her home was run. Their courtship lasted twenty months and Mr. Barrett's attitude to Browning was unrelenting hostility. Elizabeth was desperately torn between the two. Should she marry a man who would be sacrificed to a woman who could not be a real wife to him because of her invalidity or be rejected by her father and ignored by her brothers and sisters who would be ordered to have no more to do with her? She wrote:

"If I leave all for thee, wilt thou exchange
and be all to me? Shall I never miss
Home-talk and blessing and the common kiss
That comes to each in turn ....".

Elizabeth committed herself, in the autumn of 1845, to marrying Robert. Her father, of course, did not know of it. She then tried to get away to Italy for the winter hoping to meet up with Robert in Pisa but it did not work out, her father making it impossible for her to go. But now, suddenly, she told Robert she would abide by his decisions. He could get the marriage licence if he wanted to.

Everything, though, seemed to be working against them. Mr. Barrett suddenly decided that his home in Wimpole Street was to be cleaned and painted and sent his son George to find and rent a house for a month at Dover, Reigate or Tunbridge . Elizabeth and Robert both knew that by the time the month was over the onset of winter might imprison Elizabeth until the following summer. Indeed, if her health deteriorated, she might never get out of her home alive. When Elizabeth's letter arrived telling Robert the news of her father's intentions he replied the same day, Thursday, 10th September reminding her that if she were taken from London their marriage must wait another year. "You see what we have gained by waiting", he wrote, "We must be married directly and go to Italy. I shall go for a licence today and we can be married on Saturday". Robert was to rescue her from her prison at last.

Can there ever have been in England a stranger marriage than took place at St. Marylebone Parish Church on Saturday morning September 12th, 1846? Accompanied by her maid Wilson, Elizabeth was so filled with doubts and fears about whether or not her action was right that she had been afraid she would faint before she reached the street. She made it, though, down stairs with Wilson and got to a local chemist shop for some smelling salts to steady her nerves.

"I staggered so", she wrote, "that we both were afraid for the fear's sake". Then they went to a cab-stand in Marylebone Road. Just before 11 o'clock they arrived at the church.

Robert was there with his cousin, James Silverthorne and in a brief ceremony two of the greatest poets in English literature were married. No great crowds thronged against the railings outside, no society photograph recorded the wedding kiss, no confetti fell on Elizabeth's ringed curls. They parted without a word but if their hearts could have been read, what a fascinating read it would have been! Elizabeth drove alone to the house of her old Greek teacher, H.S. Boyd at Hampstead. She was kept waiting downstairs before he came to her. His surprise as she poured out her incredible news to him can only be imagined. He was delighted and euphoria broke out. Elizabeth was now joined by her two sisters, Arabel and Henrietta who had been sent for via Wilson and when Elizabeth had at last composed herself, they headed home, making a detour via the heath. She then returned to her prison in Wimpole Street. Her love for Robert and his for her, would, through their writing, soon become the property of the world.

On Saturday, 19th September accompanied by her maid, Elizabeth met Browning at Hodgson's Bookshop and took the train from Vauxhall Station and the night boat from Southampton to Le Havre. They then journeyed to Pisa arriving on October 14th and took an apartment in the Collegio Ferdinando, close to the Campo Santo of Pisa. They eventually settled in Florence in the Spring of 1847.

In time Elizabeth showed Robert the collection of 44 poems that she had written to him, before their marriage, the last sonnet dated two days before the wedding. They are amongst the greatest love poems in history and were eventually published in 1870. The thirty-eighth perhaps best describes how the lonely poetess felt at Wimpole Street when love knocked at her heart's door:

"First time he kissed me, he but only kissed
The fingers of this hand wherewith I write;
And, ever since, it grew more clean and white ...
Slow to world-greetings .... which with its Oh, list,
When angels speak. A ring of amethyst
I could not wear here, plainer to my sight,
Than that first kiss. The second passed in height
The first, and sought the forehead, and half missed,
Half falling on the hair. Oh, beyond meed!
There was the chrism of love, which love's own crown
With sanctifying sweetness, did proceed.
The third upon my lips was folded down
In perfect purple state; since when indeed,
I have been proud and said, "My love, my own."

As for her father, Elizabeth's worst fears were realised. On hearing of her marriage he wrote to her to tell her he had cut her off completely, telling her he regarded her as dead and warning her that he did not want to hear of her any more. Though she long continued to write to him, he eventually returned to her all the letters she had written to him, unopened. He took all her books out of her room and put them into store charging the rental to her. Eventually Elizabeth took her son Pen to Wimpole Street on a return visit to England, careful to go during the hours when Mr. Barrett was out. One particular day she left her son with one of his uncles in the house and Mr. Barrett suddenly appeared. "Whose child is that?", he asked. When he was told it was his daughter Elizabeth's, he immediately went into his room without a further word. When he died in April 1857 he left no message for her.

What a blessing the mean old man missed! What a joy he abrogated! What pleasure he could have given his daugher by relenting his hard line of cruelty! But it was not to be.

Elizabeth Barrett Browning died in Florence in the early hours of June 29th, 1861 and was buried in the Protestant cemetery of Florence. Shops were closed in that area of the city for her funeral and much praise was given to her work in Florentine newspapers. Into Elizabeth's Bible Robert Browning inscribed a few lines of Dante: "Thus I believe, thus I affirm, thus I am certain that from this life I shall pass to another better, there, where that lady lives of whom my soul was enamoured".

Perhaps how Robert Browning felt about Elizabeth is best described in his reaction to the publication of Edward Fitzgerald's letters in 1889. Fitzgerald was a friend of Tennyson and famous for his translation of the "Rubaiyat of Omar Khayaam". He had died in 1883. He had written on Elizabeth's death that "Mrs. Browning's death is rather a relief to me I must say ... a woman of real Genius but what is the upshot of it all? She and her Sex had better mind the Kitchen and their Children; and perhaps the Poor. Except in such things as little Novels, they only devote themselves to what Men do much better, leaving that which Men do worse or not at all".

Robert Browning's response was immediate. He wrote the following twelve line poem which was subsequently published:

To Edward Fitzgerald
"I chanced upon a new book yesterday:
I opened it, and where my finger lay
'Twixt page and uncut page, these words I read
- Some six or seven at most - and learned thereby
That you, Fitzgerald, whom by ear and eye
She never knew, "Thanked God my wife was dead".
Ay, dead! and were yourself alive good Fitz,
How to return you thanks would task my wit;
Kicking you seems the common lot of curs -
While more appropriate greeting lends you grace;

Surely to spit there glorifies your face -
Spitting - from lips once sanctified by Hers."

Robert Browning died in Venice at 10 o'clock on the evening of 12th December, 1890. The city of Venice staged a funeral service of pomp and rich colour. His coffin lay under a purple pall and with a single wreath which his son Pen had placed on it. A cortege of ornate funeral gondolas followed with the city dignitaries in their liveries down the Grand Canal and out to a temporary resting place on the burial island of San Michele. The coffin was later taken by train and boat to England and on the last day of the year 1890 in the presence of 600 ticket holders was buried in West-minster Abbey.

One of the world's great love stories had come to an end. Yet, even as Robert Browning approached death, the memory of Elizabeth was a huge inspiration when facing life's last great enemy, as his great poem 'Prospice' proves. No poem in the English language epitomises better a person's belief in resurrection after death and the joy of seeing their loved ones again:

Fear death? - to feel the fog in my throat,
The mist in my face,
When the snows begin, and the blasts denote
I am nearing the place,
The power of the night, the press of the storm,
The post of the foe;
Where he stands, the Arch Fear in a visible form,
Yet the strong man must go:
For the journey is done and the summit attained,
And the barriers fall,
Though a battle's to fight ere the guerdon be gained,
The reward of it all.
I was ever a fighter, so - one fight more,

The best and the last!
I would hate that death bandaged my eyes and forbore,
And bade me creep past.
No! let me taste the whole of it, fare like my peers
The heroes of old,
Bear the brunt, in a minute pay glad life's arrears
Of pain, darkness and cold.
For sudden the worst turns the best to the brave,
The black minute's at end,
And the elements' rage, the fiend-voices that rave,
Shall dwindle, shall blend,
Shall change, shall become first a peace out of pain,
Then a light, then thy breast,
O thou soul of my soul! I shall clasp thee again,
And with God be the rest!

The Greatest Decision Of All

Pontious Pilate's decision to have Christ crucified.

HE WAS THE MOST FAMOUS MAN IN ROMAN HISTORY - THE MAN WHO PUBLICLY WASHED HIS HANDS OFF THE BLOOD OF JESUS CHRIST. HIS DECISON WAS THE MOST MOMENTOUS ANY JUDGE OR ANY INDIVIDUAL HAS EVER MADE.

Pontius Pilate was selected by L. Aelius Sejanus , the Commander of the Praetorian Guard which was the corps of elite troops who protected the Roman Emperor and served as Rome's Government police. Nine thousand guardsmen listened and obeyed when Sejanus spoke. When he recommended Pontius Pilate as Governor of Judea the Emperor Tiberius Caesar Augustus listened too. Appointed to the post in A.D. 26 on a salary of one hundred thousand sesterces, Pilate came with the reputation of being a tough commander. He had already helped put down a mutiny in the Twelfth Legion by a combination of oratory and force and maintaining control was a high priority for any Government of a Roman Province, particularly Judea.

He cut a commanding figure indeed, even in civilian garb. His tunic sported the "angusticlavia", a narrow bordering strip of purple running the length of the garment and indicating a class second only to the Senatorial, which boasted the "laticlavia", a wider purple strip. In public, the tunic was largely covered by a toga and draping the toga bordered on an art form. Every fold had to hang properly, gracefully, and had just the right amount of purple to show from the tunic: too much would be ostentatious, too little would betray false modesty.

That Pilate intended the Romanisation of the Jews of Judea soon became very clear. His headquarters was at Caesarea. The Temple in Caesarea to Caesar Augustus, built by huge sums lavished on it by Herod was a scaled down version of the Parthenon at Athens and stood in its glory on a summit overlooking the harbour. Its Government, buildings, amphitheatre and dramatic theatre were all very impressive. Less than forty years old Caesarea lay brilliantly white in the sun surrounded by a semi-circular wall with a huge hippodrome just outside the east wall.

Pilate's immediate superior was the Imperial Legate of Syria but Pilate was nevertheless directly responsible to the Emperor for his administration of the Province. In him was vested the power of life and death. He was both Judge and Governor and was aided by a small advisory council in the skills required of a "Praesectus Judaeae". Pilate also had supreme authority in the financial administrations of Judea.

There was not a genuine Roman Army in any of the forces in Palestine. Pilate's troops were auxiliaries, non-Romans of mixed Syrian or Samaritan nationality recruited locally for Imperial service. Jews were exempt from military service because of Sabbath and dietary restrictions. Pilate's military command consisted of one ala, a cavalry company, and five infantry cohorts of five to six hundred men each, about three thousand troops in all. If a serious revolt occurred he would have had to call on help from Syria.

His 'Romanising of the Jews' policy soon ran into a massive problem. Pilate decided to dispatch the Augustan Cohort of Sebastenians to set up their winter quarters in Jerusalem at the Tower Antonia. This Cohort had put down a Zealot insurrection and the Emperor had rewarded them by permitting the Cohort to name itself "Augustan" and to carry in its identifying colours a special medallion with the Emperor's image.

Pilate knew very well that he was treading dangerous waters. Jewish law forbade the very making of images. Its law read, "You shall not make yourselves a graven image or likeness of anything that is in Heaven above or the earth beneath, or the water under the earth: you shall not bow down to them or serve them."

Pilate, knowing the sensitivity of what he was doing, ordered the Cohort to enter Jerusalem late at night. But soon the cry went up,

"Thoaivoh ne-estho be-yisroel ubi-yerusholaim", meaning, "An abomination has been committed in Israel and in Jerusalem".

Pilate had miscalculated the degree of feeling. A massive crowd descended on Caesarea demanding that the defending ensigns be withdrawn. Day and night the crowd occupied the great square adjoining the Herodian Palace where Pilate and his wife Procula lived. The crowd was determined not to leave until the ensigns were removed from the Holy City. Pilate refused to give in for he did not want to offend Caesar and six days later he set up his tribunal seat in the massive hippodrome filled now with masses of Jewish people. He argued his case and offered that anyone who showed loyalty to the Emperor by leaving Caesarea peacefully could raise their hand and be allowed through the ranks of his soldiers unmolested. Otherwise they would be cut in pieces by his troops. To Pilate's amazement the people threw themselves on the ground, laying their necks bare saying that they would willingly die rather than have their law violated.

Pilate was so moved by this incredible show of resolution that he ordered his troops to sheath their swords and let the people go free. It was a sobering lesson for him in Roman-Jewish relations. If he had any idealistic views of his Governorship before he was appointed, Pilate soon lost them.

Pilate turned back to the administration of Judea duly educated and now gave himself to a project which was dear to his heart. He wanted a basilica for his capital, one of the most popular buildings in the Mediterranean world of the time and to name it after Tiberius. If you go to Caesarea today you can see part of the corner-stone which was originally embedded in what became known as the Tiberieum. The words, partly chipped away, are in three inch lettering and are generally agreed by scholars to be: "CAESARIENS TIBERIEVM PONTIIVSPILATIVS PRAEFJECTVSIVDAEAJE DJEDIT" This means "Pontius Pilatus, Prefect of Judea, has presented the Tiberieum to the Caesarians". The stone was discovered by an Italian archaeological expedition in 1961 and is in fact the first epigraphic evidence of the existence of Pilate to be discovered. The basilica proved to be a very popular building with many Caesarians.

Soon Pilate embarked on another very popular project. He had a very laudible desire to improve the water supply in Jerusalem. Everyone thought it a wonderful idea and work began on the twenty mile aquaduct drawing water from outside pool reservoirs in the Judean countryside. Construction also began in Jerusalem to prepare to receive the new water supply. The only problem was that nobody asked where the money was coming from to pay for the aquaduct; when they found out a huge movement amongst Jews rose against Pilate. To pay for his project Pilate used the sacred Temple money. It is believed by many that he did it with the connivance of the High Priest because access to the sacred treasury in the Temple was impossible without co-operation from the Temple authorities. For Gentiles to enter the Temple meant certain death.

As the Jewish historian Josephus records it, "Pilate undertook to bring a current of water to Jerusalem, and did it with the sacred money, and derived the origin of the stream from the distance of two hundred furlongs. However, the Jews were not pleased with what had been done about this water; and many tens of thousands of people got together and made a clamour against him, and insisted that he should leave off that design. Some of them also used reproaches, and abused the man, as crowds of such people usually do. So he habited a great number of his soldiers in their habit, who carry clubs under their garments, and sent them to a place where they might surround them.

So he bid the Jews himself go away; but they boldly casting reproaches upon him, he gave the soldiers that signal which had been beforehand agreed on; laid upon them with much greater blows than Pilate had commanded them, and equally punished those that were tumultious, and those that were not: nor did they spare them in the least; and since the people were unarmed, and were caught by men who were prepared for what they were about, there were a great number of them slain by this means, and others of them ran away wounded. And thus an end was put to this sedition".

Pilate survived the enmity raised by the aquaduct incident. He even survived the fall and execution of the man who had first recommended him for his post; Sejanus was executed in A.D.32 in Rome where he had ruled as virtual Co-Emperor. Pilate continued to rule Judea fairly equably.

It was the year A.D. 33, though, which turned out to be the year that would change the course of human history and the year that would change the dating system of history as no other. Few, least of all Pilate, could have realised in its early months that a humble teacher from Galilee would change history and that what Pilate did with him would make more impact on mankind's destiny than all the Roman Emperors combined.

The trial of the Lord Jesus Christ was one of the hastiest in history. Here was no long, protracted trial lasting weeks and even months. It began in the early hours of a Friday morning, had Christ on the cross by mid-day and buried before sundown.

It was all triggered on a Thursday evening. Judas Iscariot, one of Christ's disciples, suddenly offered to lead Christ's enemies to an easy place of arrest. Those enemies scurried to get their act together and Christ was arrested where He had been praying in the Garden of Gethsamane, just outside Jerusalem's wall and He was taken immediately to the House of the notorious Annas early on Friday morning. Not all Jewish leaders in history, thank God, were like Annas. He was, to say the least, a real snake in the grass.

In ancient Israel a High Priest was a High Priest for life but when the Romans came the office went to the highest bidder and to the person who would willingly co-operate with the Roman authorities. The High Priest was, in fact, at that time, an arch collaborator. Annas had been High Priest from A.D. 6-15 and had been deposed by the former Prefect of Judea but in the intervening years four of his sons- in-law held the office and Caiaphas who was the present incumbent was a son-in-law. He was, in every way, the power behind the throne.

It is not hard to see why Annas arranged that Jesus should be brought to him, first. Annas had made his money disgracefully. When sacrifices were brought to the temple they had to be examined and passed without blemish. The inspectors under Annas's authority found plenty of flaws, even when there weren't any. The worshipper was then shown where he could buy victims already passed by Annas' inspectors at the temple booths. It all looked very pious and seemed extremely holy but the plain fact was that a pair of doves could cost three times as much inside the temple as outside! The temple booths were called the "Bazaars of Annas". He had amassed a fortune.

The bound and arrested Christ now stood before this notorious leader. He who knew no sin and did no sin and in whose mouth was no guile now looked into the eyes of the man Hell-bent on having Him done to death. This was the One who, "Found in the temple those who sold oxen and sheep and doves and the moneychangers. When he had made a whip of cords, He drove them all out of the temple, with the sheep and the oxen and poured out the changers' money and overturned the tables.

And He said to those who sold doves, 'Take those things away! Do not make my Father's house a house of merchandise!'". Christ now looked into the gloating eyes of the man who is delighted to have him in his grasp at last.

We must never forget in Western civilisation that when our forefathers were pagans the Jewish people were honouring and witnessing to the glory of God. To them were given on Mount Sinai the moral codes of God for our lives which, in due course, changed civilisation. Yet, sadly, as in all peoples there were those who abused those laws and Annas was certainly one of them. Jewish law insists that a person must be asked no questions which by answering would cause the prisoner to admit any kind of guilt. Annas broke this law. When Christ gently pointed this out to Him, an officer slapped Him across the face. So much for Annas' sense of justice.

Christ was then sent to the acting High Priest, Caiaphas. Witness after false witness was arranged before Christ and all of them broke down in their evidence. Out of sheer shame they had to be dismissed. Eventually Caiaphas could stand it no longer and burst out, putting Christ under oath, "I adjure you by the living God that you tell us whether you are the Christ, the son of the Blessed".

Christ who had been silent until now, could not hold His peace without being inconsistent with the whole tenor of His life and ministry. Amid the breathless silence of the court He said without a falter, "I am". Caiaphas was delighted; now he had him. For a man to claim to be the Son of God would make him guilty of blasphemy and he must be put to death according to Jewish law. The High Priest tore his clothes in a show of pious horror at what he claimed to be Christ's crime and then they condemned Christ to death.

There was now an interval and in the interval the men who held Jesus mocked Him, beat Him and spat on His face. The Saviour showed no retaliation. Though one word from those pale compressed lips would have led them all low in death or could have drawn back the veil of eternity and shown legions of angels waiting impatiently to burst on the impious scene. Yet, amazingly, He said nothing.

Christians have often, in history, blamed the Jews for killing Christ and even, horror of horrors, said that the Holocaust was a punishment for what they did. Such a disgraceful view is certainly not the view of the New Testament. It states categorically that "Christ died for our sins"; it was not just Jewish sin that nailed Christ to the cross, it was all our sin. As Isaiah had written a long time before in his prophecy, "He was wounded for our transgressions, He was bruised for our iniquities; the chastisement for our peace was upon Him and by his stripes we are healed. All we like sheep have gone astray; we have turned, everyone, to his own way, and the Lord has laid on Him the iniquity of us all". Those Jewish leaders were far from being sinners beyond all others; we all have the same evil human heart. Of course, the leaders of the nation were involved in His crucifixion but many hundreds of thousands of Jews living across the Mediterranean and beyond only heard about the crucifixion months or even years after it had occurred. Such people cannot be said to have been responsible for the awful deed.

Those who were, though, led the Saviour away to the Jewish Council and, probably within a few minutes, had Him condemned. The next step was, though, more difficult for them. The Roman authorities from one end of their Empire to the other resolutely kept the power of execution to themselves; in practical terms the sentence of death could only be given by the hand of the Roman Prefect of Judea and his name was Pontius Pilate.

To say that Pilate had problems with the Jewish authorities in the past was an understatement and in a very real sense he had lived up to his name. Pilatus meant "armed with a javelin". The "pilum" or javelin was a balanced missile six feet long, half wooden handle and half pointed iron shaft, which Roman legionaires hurled at their enemies with devastating effect. It has been pointed out that the "pilum", in fact, had made the Empire possible. So now they took Christ to the man behind whom stood the force and power of Rome. They knew very well that Pilate would never have him executed on a religious charge of blasphemy. He would have told them, as he eventually did, to take Christ away and settle their own private religious quarrels among themselves.

In the end they produced a charge of rebellion and political insurrection, accusing Christ of claiming to be a king. They knew their accusation was a lie and in truth a person has no case at all who has to support it by a lie. They even said, "We have no king but Caesar" which must have been a statement that took Pilate's breath away. When the Romans first came to Judea and set up taxation procedures there was a vicious rebellion because Jews insisted that God alone was their king and that they would pay Him their tribute and Him alone. The truth was that these men were prepared to abandon every principle they ever had in order to have Christ eliminated.

Was there, though, ever in history, a scene like that which now faced Pilate on that infamous Spring morning? The sun was climbing in the sky and soon it would be very hot. Suddenly a remarkable crowd started filling into the esplanade before the Praetorium; the Praetorium was the temporary headquarters or Judgment Hall of the Roman Governor while he was in Jerusalem. It was, in fact, actually Herod's palace adjacent to the Jewish temple. There were priests and guardsmen, Scribes and Pharisees and a huge crowd which could be best described as, for the main part, a rabble. Christ was now being presented not before a religious court but a Government court; it was not a religious trial now, it was a civil trial.

Of course the men who presented Christ would not themselves enter the Praetorium, that would prevent them eating Passover, that would cause them to be ritually defiled. They were, as Jesus Christ had said in an earlier sermon, straining at a gnat and swallowing a camel. Pilate came out of the Praetorium and asked what accusation they brought against their prisoner. They sarcastically told him that if Christ were not an evil-doer they would not have delivered him for judgment in the first place. Pilate then asked them to judge Christ according to their law but they told him they were after a death sentence and only he could deliver it. They had gone as far as they could.

Pilate then called Christ into the Praetorium. The Roman Prefect was now face to face with God Incarnate though he didn't know it. "Are you", he asked, "the King of the Jews?". He had obviously now learned the accusation that had been brought against Christ. "Are you speaking for yourself on this or did others tell you about me?", replied the Saviour. It was a very haunting and searching question. Pilate had never met such a personality before and answered, angrily; "Am I a Jew? Your own nation and the chief priests have delivered you to me. What have you done?".

What had He done, indeed? He had put stars in space, spoke and worlds were formed, even now He held Pilate's breath in His hand. "My Kingdom is not of this world", answered Christ, "If my Kingdom were of this world, my servants would fight, so I should not be delivered to the Jews; but now my kingdom is not from here".

Pilate obviously thought that if Christ claimed to have a kingdom then He must be a King. "Are you a King then?", he asked. "You rightly say that I am a King. For this cause I was born, and for this cause I have come into the world, that I should bear witness to the truth. Everyone who is of the truth hears my voice". Christ obviously claimed Kingship in the realm of truth. It was the Roman Governor who was now arrested. Many were the corners he had come around, many were the things he knew of an Empire based on force, but, a kingdom based on truth, that was something else. "What is truth?", he asked. Was he jesting? No. He never felt less like jesting in all his life. He was world weary and he was basically saying if the nature of Christ's Kingdom was truth, then that Kingdom hadn't much of a chance of realisation in the world that he knew.

Pilate then went out to the crowd and pronounced the official sentence of acquittal. "I find no fault in this Man", he said, "but you have a custom that I should release someone to you at the Passover. Do you therefore want me to release to you the King of the Jews?". Then they all cried again, saying, "Not this man, but Barabbas!". Everyone in the crowd, of course, knew that Barabbas was a robber.

The trial of the Lord Jesus then took an appallingly wicked turn. Pilate who had just acquitted Christ now took Him back into the Praetorium and had Him scourged. Among the Romans either rods were used or whips. In Christ's case it was a whip, the thongs of which were weighted with jagged pieces of bone or metal to make the blow more effective.

The number of blows was left to the whim of the Commanding Officer. His victims, tied to a stake with back bared to the tormentors, generally fainted from the resultant lacerations, or even died. Scourging was forbidden to Roman citizens being generally reserved for slaves or those condemned to death. How very moving are the words of the Bible that tell us of what followed the scourging. "And the soldiers twisted a crown of thorns and put it on His head, and they put on Him a purple robe. Then they said, 'Hail, King of the Jews!' and they struck Him with their hands. Pilate then went out again, and said to them, 'Behold, I am bringing Him out to you, that you may know that I find no fault in Him'. Then Jesus came out, wearing the crown of thorns and the purple robe. And Pilate said to them, 'Behold the man!'".

Why had Pilate violated all justice in having Christ scourged and yet deep down in his heart he knew Christ was innocent? It would seem that he had within him the hope that the scourged, lacerated and thorn-crowned and bruised and bleeding man would appeal to their pity. But they would have none of it and the chief priests and officers cried out, "Crucify! Crucify!" Pilate then said, "Take Him yourselves, and crucify Him; for I find no fault in Him". He knew very well that they could not do it but he was mocking them. He thought he had found a way out.

Christ's enemies now tried another tact. "We have a law", they said, "And by that law He ought to die because He made Himself to be the Son of God". The truth was out at last. This was their quarrel with Christ and the pagan Pilate now found fear gripping him. He entered into the

Praetorium again with Christ. "Where are you from?", he said to Christ. Perplexed, harassed, worried and now frightened, he had asked one of the most profound questions a human being could ever ask of Christ. He had in fact asked God Incarnate where He came from.

It is a question that we, even in these last few years of the twentieth century and facing the years of a new century, must again ask. The Bible's answer is categorical. "In the beginning was the Word and the Word was with God, and the Word was God. He was in the beginning with God. All things were made through Him, and without Him nothing was made that was made. In Him was life, and the life was the light of men". To Pilate's question, though, Jesus said nothing.

"Do you not speak to me?", said Pilate. "Do you not know that I have power to crucify you, and power to release you?". On a human level he was right but Christ now revealed His sense of authority that rose far higher than any of Caesar's authority; "You would have no authority against Me except it were given you from above. Therefore the one who delivered me to you has the greater sin". Christ was apportioning guilt. Caiaphas who had sinned against the spiritual had the greater sin.

It was very obvious that up until this moment Pilate had done his best to try to find a way to release Christ. If anyone studies the Scriptural account of the trial of Jesus Christ, Pilate had gone in and out of the Praetorium seven times. It showed his threshing about in mind and heart and soul and spirit to try to come to a decision. Even his wife had warned him to have nothing to do with the righteous Christ for she had suffered many things that day in a dream because of Him. He must now, though, make up his mind. He must now either crucify Christ or free Him.

What was it that made Pilate decide in the end? It was a statement hurled at Him by the Jews in the crowd; "If you let this man go, you are not Caesar's friend", they said, "Whoever makes himself a King speaks against Caesar". That decided it. It was political blackmail on the part of the Jewish leadership. There never was a more hypocritical word spoken because they despised Caesar but it suited their purposes and Pilate now saw his job on the line. They were really saying that if he freed Christ the Sanhedrin of the Jews would send a delegation to Tiberius to bring a charge of criminal neglect of duty for failing to punish someone who committed "maiestas", i.e. setting himself up as a subversive counter-King to the Roman Emperor. As Pilate's momentous decision had hung in the balance, there is no question that his mind was duelling with the fact that freeing Christ could lead to loss not only of his office, but his political career or even life itself if the charge of treason were sustained. For Pilate the trial was over. His office and his political career mattered more to him than freeing a just man.

He did try, though, just once more, to release Jesus for we are told that he brought Jesus out and sat down in the judgment seat in a place that is called The Pavement, but in Hebrew, Gabbatha .... and he said to the Jews, "Behold your King!", but they cried out, "Away with Him, away with Him! Crucify Him! " Pilate said to them, "Shall I crucify your King?". The chief priests answered, "We have no king but Caesar!". So it was that Pilate called for water and washed his hands before the multitude, saying, "I am innocent of the blood of this just person. You see to it". So he delivered Christ to them to be crucified and they took Jesus and led Him away.

What happened to Pilate in the end? History tells us that he finally overreached himself in A.D. 36 when he was responsible for the massacre of Samaritans and was ordered by Vitellius, then President of Syria, to return to Rome to answer in person before the Emperor the accusation of the Samaritans. Vitellius sent Marcellus, a friend of his, to take Pilate's position in the affairs of Judea. So it was that Pilate hurried to Rome in obedience to the orders of Vitellius but before he ever got there, Tiberius died. We never hear of Pilate again, except in legend.

What is the verdict of history on Pilate? The verdict of history is that despite what he did to Jesus, he lost his job anyway. It reminds us of Christ's haunting words that no person can serve two masters. Pilate had looked into the eyes of Truth but he preferred prestige; he had been face to face with the Saviour of his soul but he wanted temporal benefits rather than future spiritual ones. Of all the things he said during the trial of Jesus Christ, there is one question which has echoed through the centuries that have followed. It comes to all of our hearts in every generation. In a very real sense Christ is still on trial and Pilate's question is as relevant as ever. He asked, "What shall I do then with Jesus which is called Christ?" On our answer to that question hangs our eternal destiny.

What is this story of infinite grace
That reaches right into my heart?
What is this love of priceless degree
In which my soul has a part?

Can it be true that the Maker of stars
Entered a Virgin's womb?
And lay in a manger in Bethlehem
And cried in the lantern's loom.

Who is this lad in the Temple's court
Talking to men of renown?
Is this God in a visible form
As His parents search around?

Can those hands in a carpenter's shop
Be hands that Life unfurled?
Can those lips so guileless and kind
Be lips that will judge the world?

Tell me if the man who lifts that child
Can lift my burdens too?
Tell me if He who raises the dead
Can make my life anew?

A Shepherd is He who saves His sheep
From the marauding power of the wolf?
Could I too be saved from the wrath to come,
Tell me, where is the proof?

There is but one answer to all I ask
And it stood on a skull-like hill,
Where men gambled and cursed and mocked
And said, "Is this His Father's will?".

There is the peace my soul longs for,
There is the joy I seek,
The death of the Saviour brings life to me,
I gladly fall at His feet.

The cross of Christ is the secret for me,
That will last my whole life long,
And all of its themes will for ever be,
My glory, my boast and my song.

The Three Lights

Some spiritual guidelines for the decision-maker.

WE HAVE TRACED IN THIS BOOK SOME DECISIONS THAT HAVE HAD MOMENTOUS EFFECTS ON HISTORY. YET, IN A VERY REAL SENSE, HISTORY IS MADE UP OF ALL OUR DECISIONS.

Good decisions bring a rich harvest in our lives and bad decisions bring a poor harvest. Are there, then, spiritual guidelines which will help to guide us in our decision making? There certainly are because guidance, from a Biblical standpoint, is all about making good decisions. Let's look at some of those spiritual guidelines available to all who, in repentance and faith, follow Jesus Christ.

Many years ago a famous Christian writer was travelling from an Irish port to Holyhead on the Welsh coast. He was standing on the bridge with the Captain, chatting to him about the voyage. "How do you know when you are on course for Holyhead?", he asked him. "When I approach the port", replied the Captain, "I see three lights on the horizon. When I manoeuvre my ship to a position where I can make the three lights, one light, I am on course for Holyhead". The writer lifted his pen when he got home and wrote of how believers have three lights which are always on the horizon of their lives to guide them. When they find those three lights are one light, they can be sure they are on course for making a good decision in their lives within the will of God.

The first light is the light of the Scriptures. If the Scriptures are against what you are going to do, then don't do it. They have spoken out clearly on a multitude of issues from marriage to communication, from neighbourhood relations to handling enemies, from running a business to life's true priorities, from being a good parent to finding the way to Heaven. If the Scriptures have spoken clearly and directly on an issue, then we need no further guidance on the issue; we simply obey the Scriptures.

There are, of course, other things on which the Scriptures have not spoken clearly. They have not told us, for example, whether to go to the

Seychelles or London for our holidays, have they? They have not told us whether to wear blue socks or red socks, today. They have not told us which specific person to marry or not to marry. They have not spelled out which particular house to buy or not to buy, which particular flat to rent or which college or university to study in, or what particular job to take or refuse. In such situations, God uses another light on the horizon called the light of circumstance.

Suddenly we find ourselves in a particular circumstance and wonder what on earth is going on. Our very lives at times may seem to be caving in and it almost appears as if God has forgotten us. Do you not think Joseph wondered what God was up to when his brothers threw him in a pit? Do you think, had you been talking to him, he would have said, "It's wonderful down here, I am on my way to becoming Prime Minister of Egypt?". Do you think as his brothers sold him to the Ishmaelites who took him as a slave to Egypt, that he had any idea that the day would come when Pharoah would say to Joseph, "Without your consent no man may lift his hand or foot in all the land of Egypt?" As Joseph entered into prison because a very evil woman had lied about him, he did not know that the prison was God's highway to the palace! Circumstances in our lives are often dark, but, if we only realised it, they are God's light in the path of guidance to lead us on to the next important phase of our lives.

The Scripture tells us that "On the first day of the week Mary Magdelene came to the tomb early, while it was still dark". She found the Saviour's tomb, empty, and thought it was the darkest day of her life. Frantically she went searching for His body, telling Peter in despair what had happened. She even found what she thought was the gardener and said, "Sir, if you have carried Him away, tell me where you have laid Him and I will come and take Him away".

Superbly, of course, what Mary thought was the darkest day of her life turned out to be the best day of her life. In fact, it turned out to be the best day in the history of the entire world. The supposed gardener turned out to be the Risen Christ! The greatest news the world ever heard came out of a graveyard! Don't, then, panic when circumstances seem to threaten. God uses circumstances as a light to guide you.

Just as he was having his toughest day,
And Goliath was coming with a lot to say,
And Israel was silent, come what may,
God was working it out for good!

Just as they thought it would never come,
And three walls surrounded Babylon,
And the people of God were sick for home,
God was working it out for good!

Just when the times were dark and dread,
And the Assyrian hosts by a fiend were led,
The angel moved and the foe lay dead,
God was working it out for good!

Just when they thought their case was lost,
They heard a knock and said, "'It's a ghost,'
But Peter arrived when they needed him most,
God was working it out for good!

Just stop today and bow your knee,
Though you're ready to scream and ready to flee,
Lift your heart to Him and say with me,
God is working it out for good!

On their own, of course, circumstances as a guide can be dangerous. We read in the Scriptures that Jonah, the rebellious prophet, found his circumstances very conducive. The wind was in the right direction. The ship's captain was amiable. Jonah had money in his pocket. He said, in effect, "Viva Espana!" and set sail for the Spanish coast. Circumstances looked fine but the Word of the Lord had already told Jonah to go to Nineveh. It took very frightening circumstances to arise in order to bring Jonah to see that when God guides us, the light of circumstances and the light of His Word must be one before we set sail on a new phase of our lives.

The third light is the light of "the peace of God". There is a great difference between "peace with God" and the "peace of God". When a person receives Christ as Saviour, they are justified by faith and immediately have, "peace with God through our Lord Jesus Christ". That means they are no longer at enmity with God, they are now at peace with Him. All Hell cannot remove a person from that position. The "peace of God", though, is different. It is conditional. "In every thing, by prayer and supplication with thanksgiving, let your requests be made known to God and the peace of God which surpasses all understanding will guard your hearts and minds through Christ Jesus", says the Bible.

When the believer requests something from God with a thankful heart for what God has already given them, then "the peace of God" the tranquility of God's own eternal being, the peace which God Himself has, the calm serenity that characterises His very nature, will become theirs. Yet, we must always remember, it is conditional. It comes by prayer and an attitude of thankfulness. God's peace is able to produce better results than human planning, and is more effective for removing anxiety than any intellectual effort or power of reasoning. It "rises above every mind". It will protect the believer's heart and mind, i.e. the believer's entire inner being; emotions, affections, thoughts, and, vitally important, all their moral choices. This is what believers mean when they say, "Do you have peace about it?". They mean, "Does a sense of the peace of God fill your mind and heart about what you are going to decide to do in a given circumstance?" Even if the whole world is shoving you to do something, if you do not have a sense of the peace of God about what you are doing, don't let them budge you.

So it is that when faced with a decision in life, a Christian must make sure that the light of the Word of God, the light of circumstance, and the light of the peace of God, are one light. If one of these three is missing, wait until it comes into line and then proceed. You will find that God's lights of guidance, if followed, will never lead you on to the rocks. Trust Him.

Despite the lights of guidance that God provides along the voyage of life, a lot of people are very up-tight about knowing God's will in their lives. In fact many are full of fear and guilt on the subject. Why? It all stems from the fact that they think they have missed the will of God for their lives. You know the type; "God called me to go up the Amazon as a missionary when I was 22 but I didn't go and now the rest of my Christian life is a failure". There is another fear many believers experience. It is not that they have deliberately disobeyed God's call, it is that they fear they have, unintentionally, misread it. They fear they have an innate lack of ability to read God's signs of guidance correctly. They treat God's will as being like an itinerary drawn up by a travel agent. As long as we follow the agent's instructions and be in the right place, at the right time, boarding each aircraft, bus or boat as indicated, then all is well. But miss one of the pre-planned connnections and the itinerary is ruined.

Many people feel that a revised plan can only be second-best compared with the original programme. Is this your view of God's will for your life? Is this your view of God? If you miss a connection here or there along the way, do you really think God cannot bring you back to His purpose for you? Have you forfeited your usefulness? It is worth asking whether or not you would treat your own child in such a manner. Why then do believers think their Heavenly Father, who is love itself, would treat them, His children, differently? Let's look at some characters in Scripture who made a mess of things in their decision-making. It is a fascinating meditation.

Take Abraham, for an example. Abraham panicked on the path of God's will and fled to Egypt, lying to Pharoah that Sarah his wife was his sister to protect himself. God had given Abraham great promises that He would guide and direct him but he forgot about those promises and lived on his wits. He was thrown out of Egypt by Pharoah. What hope would you have given that Abraham would become a legend and an inspiration in history as a man of staggering faith in God? None! Yet, he did become just that. God got him back on track and he became known as the Father of the Faithful.

Think about Moses. A meditation on the life of Moses, after murdering an Egyptian in order, he thought, to further God's cause will not lead you to the conclusion that God made sure he became a second rate leader because of his disastrous mistakes. He became one of the greatest leaders in all of history.

What do you make of the con-man, Jacob? Manipulative, supplanting, self-centred Jacob made sure, by foul means, that things went his way. Look at what God did through him; he became a "Prince" with God. His disastrous beginning did not ensure a disastrous end. Could we have a greater example in all of Scripture of a person who, despite much error, eventually fulfilled the will of God for his life than Samson?

Quite frankly, Samson disobeyed virtually every rule in God's book. Yet, the angel told his mother that he would "begin to deliver Israel from the Philistines". Did he?

What is your view of Samson? A big lout? A he-man with a she-weakness? A man who fooled about with God's gifts to him and who was eventually discarded by God? This is not God's ultimate view. He certainly did deliberately disobey God's instructions to him on many occasions but for many years he judged Israel successfully. His failures are highlighted by God for our learning, but, when Samson died, he effected a greater deliverance from the enemies of God's people by his death than even by his life! There was no doubt that the enemies of God eventually knew where Samson's strength originated. He got back on track, all right, with a vengeance! Did Peter not disobey God's will for his life? Most certainly . He denied to a teenage girl that he even knew the Christ. He who had said he would die for the Saviour miserably failed to live for Him on the night when the Saviour needed him most. Was he thrown aside by the Lord? Did he become a God's second-best? Have you read any of Peter's New Testament letters recently? There are fewer passages of Scripture more inspiring for people going through trouble. Was he restored to God's purpose for his life? Fewer have known a more complete restoration. A few weeks later he was leading thousands to faith in Christ. The Saviour met Peter by the lake, warmed him by a fire and fed him with fish and pointed him to the way back. Peter discovered that neither his sin, nor his temper or mood, nor the passage of time had lessened Christ's love for him nor dampened Christ's desire to see Peter live out God's purposes for his life.

So, if you have made a bad decision or sinned in disobeying God's clear instructions to you, it is categorically not the end. God knew that we were failures before He took us on. He has promised never to leave us nor forsake us, no matter who else does. He told the erring Abraham, "I am your shield and your exceeding great reward". God loves us and is not going to put us on the scrap-heap or the shelf just because we have erred. It is true that sin has its earthly consequences and that stupid and silly decisions have repercussions but if there is repentance on our part and willingness to try again, God can restore and use us.

Let us be reminded of a wild, dissolute and drunken youth who went one evening to a home Bible Study amongst a few belivers in Germany.

He got converted to Christ. Fervent in his faith but pretty empty in Scriptural knowledge he thought that God wanted him to be a missionary. Having a knowledge of gambling on horses, he went to a racecourse and put a bet on a horse. "If it wins, Lord", he prayed, "I will know you want me to be a missionary!". If you had been passing that racecourse you wouldn't have given much hope for that young man ever finding God's will in his life, would you? His name was George Muller and he became one of the greatest Christians in 19th century British history!

There are a lot of people, of course, who think that there is Divine intervention in the life of a person every time he or she has a major decision to make. It is worth asking whether or not God intervenes every time we have to make decisions. Let's take it on the human level, first. Parents in training children do not intervene in every decision their children make in life, do they? Certainly not. Why? Because if they did, their children would never grow up. They would never learn to make responsible decisions in life if they were not given freedom to make some earlier in life. A parent intervening all the time would create a very spoilt child bereft of the social skills needed for balanced living. Such an approach would also create a child who would be eventually seriously flawed in any decision-making process in their life.

What would any wise parent do in order to aid their child to be a good decision-maker? They would set their child limits to observe. Obviously a child would not be allowed to do whatever it wanted because, out of lack of experience for a start, it might choose a line of action whose consequences the child would simply not be capable of knowing. To allow it complete freedom would bring incalculable disaster. Yet, drawing from the wisdom of his or her parents and their example, and observing the limits set, a child can be allowed freedom to make decisions. By such a process the child slowly but surely grows up to be a responsible adult. Let's take these guidelines to the spiritual level. God wants His children to grow up responsibly. He wants them to be able to use their minds and exercise their spiritual muscles and make good decisions in their lives. Though, He too sets limits to observe. The Bible shows very clearly what God hates to see in His image bearers. So we, by His grace, can avoid those things that God hates. Drawing, then, from God's wisdom and observing the limits He sets as revealed in the Scriptures and having His example to follow as reflected in the life of the Lord Jesus while He was here on earth, we are allowed to use our minds to make good decisions and so grow up as responsible people.

There is, in Scripture, a very gripping and instructive example of those guidelines we have just been thinking about. It concerns a very important pivot in the history of the Christian church, namely, the story of how Paul was guided to first bring the Gospel of Jesus Christ to Europe. Consider the scene. God wants to bring Paul to Europe to sow a very important seed whose harvest we are enjoying today. Did He intervene in Paul's life with a flash of lightning from the sky or have some Scripture verse to burden him heavily to shift him from the Middle East to Europe? Not on this occasion. We read in Acts 15; 36 that "After some days Paul said to Barnabas, 'Let us now go back and visit our brethren in every city where we have preached the Word of the Lord and see how they are doing' ". What were Paul and Barnabas doing? They were simply responding to God's standing order that shepherds of God's flock should care for and feed their sheep. Paul and Barnabas needed no special guidance for that any more than Germans need a letter from their Chancellor, or the British need a letter from their Queen or Americans need a letter from their President every week to tell them to pay their taxes! As a friend of mine once put it, "What mother, in normal circumstances, would earnestly pray to the Lord for direct special guidance whether it was His will that she give her baby its breakfast?".

The plain fact is that we don't need special Divine guidance in a whole lot of areas of activity in our lives. The standing order to the Christian is to be a good citizen, a good neighbour, to spread the Gospel, to care for family and friends, etc. So, let's get on with the standing orders, just like Paul did and if we need special intervention from God to guide us, we will get it. Paul did. As he went to encourage the churches he had planted, God intervened with special guidance, twice. Yet, notice that it was with negative intervention, telling him not to go to Asia or Bithynia (See Acts 16; 6-7).

It is vital to understand that all of this time Paul and those friends with him were never given advance information as to where God was eventually leading them! Paul didn't know that when God stopped him going to preach in Asia and then in Bithynia, that the whole purpose was to get him to go to Philippi. Moses' parents didn't get advance information that when they put their baby in the ark of bulrushes and floated it in the Nile, that Pharoah's daughter would find the child, adopt him and that God would get Moses to eventually lead the children of Israel across the wilderness!

You don't get advance information from God that when you lose a job, or are passed over for promotion, or are sidelined by your friends through no fault of your own, that it will lead to a wonderful goal God has for you in the future. Everything that happens to us is not necessarily good, but it always works together for good. Special Divine guidance may not necessarily let you know where you are being led. It may be just to keep you "on track" on the line of obeying God's standing orders.

Eventually Paul and his friends arrive in Troas. We are not told how long it took them to get there but it must have been a very long journey taking up a considerable amount of time. They got special Divine guidance in the form of a vision which Paul had in the night. A man from Macedonia stood and pleaded with Paul saying, "Come over to Macedonia and help us". Did Paul jump out of bed in the morning and say, "Right men, we are off to Europe?". He did not. He first of all talked over what he had experienced with his friends and the Scripture says that they " concluded" (i.e. inferred) that the Lord had called them to Macedonia. It is, therefore, a very good idea to discuss with Godly and caring friends those things which you consider to be special Divine guidance in your life. Paul and his party eventually arrived in Philippi and the Lord opened Lydia's heart to the Gospel. She in turn opened her home to Paul and Silas and God in turn opened the Continent of Europe to the best news it ever had.

What do we learn, then, from this Scriptural story to help us in the nitty gritty of seeking God's guidance for our daily lives? We learn that if we were never allowed to decide anything but were always controlled by constant interventions from God directly guiding us, we would never grow up to be mature believers.

When God's plans or our needs require it, God can and often does intervene with special guidance. This may be in the form of a dramatic intervention or maybe through a circumstance such as bumping into a friend, receiving a telephone call, reading a magazine article or crossing a certain street. God's doors swing on little hinges. God sets limits for our behaviour by showing us in the Bible the things that He hates. If we, by His grace, avoid these, our decisions within these limits will bring glory to Him and help us to mature. God never by-passes our moral or spiritual judgments. If God broke your mind, you would be as a jellyfish or a vegetable. He helps you by His Holy Spirit to do His will. When a good door closes, God opens a better one. Consider these examples.

Some years ago the late Bishop Taylor-Smith was travelling by railway from somewhere in Northern England to somewhere South. He missed a connection at Leeds, Yorkshire, and found he had two hours to wait. As always, in such circumstances, he accepted this as "permissive providence" and prayed for guidance, asking if God had some special purpose in allowing the delay. Strolling from the station to the big square outside, he sat on a form, and noticed that its only other occupant was a middle-aged man who looked the very picture of misery. Shabbily dressed, bent shoulders, head drooped down on his hands, he took no notice whatever of the burly clergyman who now sat near him. Still counting on guidance, the Bishop said, "You seem to be in some deep trouble". "Yes, I sure am", the man muttered without lifting his eyes. "I am at the end of things, Mister". He coughed hoarsely, then added, "Maybe you will not believe me, Mister, but tonight I am going to end everything; and I am just having this last sit out here".

"But is there no-one can help you?", asked the Bishop. "Nobody", came the dejected reply.

After a pause, head sagging still lower, the man added, "Begging your pardon, stranger, there is just one man who could have helped me, if I could have found him; but I haven't seen him these fifteen years, and I have no notion where he is". "Who is he?", asked the Bishop.

"He was my Army Padre in France during the war, but I clean forget his name". "Which regiment and company were you in? What battles were you in? ", enquired the Bishop. The man slowly told him, still without looking up. Then, stretching out his hand, and gently lifting the man's head up, the Bishop said, "Well, my brother, look at me. Your man is right here; I was that Padre; and after all these years God has sent me to help you here and now!" Would anybody stubbornly pretend that such happenings are mere coincidences? Surely this is the operation of real Divine guidance in and through consecrated individuals. What channels of blessing we might become if we were only living such guided lives! Don't think, though, that leading such a guided life brings wonderful consequences immediately. Let's look at another example.

Situated in its own beautiful grounds near England's Lake District sits Capernwray Hall which houses the famous Christian Conference Centre and Bible School. A while back the Directors of Capernwray Hall bought a castle in Austria as a Holiday and Conference Centre and God richly blessed them in their work there. They wondered why things were so especially blessed until one day they found a Bible belonging to the man who had built the castle. He had written a prayer on the fly-leaf of the Bible asking God to use the castle to His glory.

Though the man had done his best to serve the Lord, holding services in the castle, and witnessing to others, he was severely persecuted throughout his Christian life. He died, heartbroken and with no evident results from his faithful service. He seemed to have been on the wrong road of service. Was he? Not at all. God answered his prayer when the Capernwray folks moved in. The significant thing, though, was that they discovered the Bible and its written prayer to be 700 years old!

Are you discouraged on the path of doing what you know to be the will of God? Have you had clear guidance and sought all these months, and maybe even years, to do it? Is there no great sign that you are being successful? Who said that you were to be judged on outward success, encouraging as it is when it comes? Surely what you are called to be is to be faithful. In the end, doing God's will is good, perfect and acceptable, though, at the time you are carrying it out it appears to be anything but scintillating.

To bring our book to a conclusion, let us consider, finally, the role of the Bible in decision-making. It is an amazing fact how few people actually read the Scriptures. In the Dark Ages, copies of the Scriptures were chained to the pulpit in the secret language of the clergy and the public were kept ignorant of the life-changing nature of its truths. Men like Tyndale were burnt alive for trying to get the Scriptures into the hands of the common people. In those days Biblical ignorance was forced. Now, in our day, it is voluntary. In fact the more versions of Scripture we have, the less the Bible is read.

In a school, here in the West, a teacher quizzed a group of college-bound High School pupils on the Bible. Here are some of the answers he received.

Jesus was baptised by Moses.
Sodom and Gomorrah were lovers.
Jezebel was Ahab's donkey.
The New Testament Gospels were written by Matthew, Mark, Luther and John.
Eve was created from an apple.
The most hilarious, if sad, answer to the question, "What was Golgotha?" was, "Golgotha was the name of the giant who slew the Apostle David."

Despite the fact that millions neglect the Scriptures, it does not take away the reality that there is no other place where better guidance can be found for everyday living. To move away from the pages of Scripture is to enter the wastelands of subjectivity. The Bible is a divinely provided map containing directions and markings to guide people to the true order for family or nation. To ignore its teachings leads to moral and spiritual shipwreck. So, why not get a "One Year Bible" which divides the Scriptures into readings which will take you from Genesis to Revelation in one year. No matter where you are, and no matter who you have got to meet, no matter what deadlines crop up, why not spend twenty minutes in the Scriptures every day? It will not be long before you feel the enormous benefit of your reading.

There is of course, nothing magical in reading the Scriptures. They need to be obeyed and you need to know the author, which is possible through Jesus Christ. We know very well that professional religious types have been merely reading the Scriptures and disobeying them for centuries. It is obviously important that the Scriptures are obeyed and the

Saviour they present, trusted. Yet if you read the Scriptures regularly, the benefits are incalculable. If you doubt it just check out these points from Psalm 119. They spell out the benefits very clearly:

1. God's Word establishes my way. (v.5)
2. God's Word purifies my life. (v.9-11)
3. God's Word gives me counsel. (v.24)
4. God's Word removes everything false in me. (v.29)
5. God's Word produces reverence for God. (v.38)
6. God's Word increases my courage. (v.46)
7. God's Word comforts me in afflictions. (v.50)
8. God's Word guards me from panic. (v.61-62)
9. God's Word teaches me discernment and knowledge. (v.65-66)
10. God's Word makes me resourceful. (v.79)
11. God's Word cultivates patience. (v.87)
12. God's Word keeps me spiritually recharged. (v.93)
13. God's Word accelerates my understanding. (v.98-100)
14. God's Word creates a joyful heart. (v.111)
15. God's Word sustains me when I feel helpless. (v.116)
16. God's Word enables me to honour what is right and hate what is wrong. (v.128)
17. God's Word causes me to walk in the truth. (v.133)
18. God's Word surrounds me with delight in spite of difficulty. (v.143)
19. God's Word develops the discipline of prayer. (v.147)
20. God's Word rescues me when I am defenceless. (v.152-154)
21. God's Word fills me with praise without and peace within. (v.164-165)
22. God's Word draws me back when I stray. (v.176)

It is a fact that nothing else will do for you what the Scriptures will. It is vital that we make place for them in our daily lives. As for helping us in our decision-making, which, we have discovered is the main thrust of Divine guidance, there is a grid of some Biblical principles and some checkpoints which together constitute the way of wisdom for all who follow the Lord.

1. THERE ARE INSTRUCTIONS TO HEED

There is obviously no point in asking God for guidance if we refuse to obey the instructions He has already given in the Scriptures. For example, the Scriptures say that "If I regard iniquity in my heart the Lord will not hear me". (Psalm 66; 18). This means that if I hug grudges, enjoy tittle-tattle, nurse jealousies, pass on gossip, lead an undisciplined, self-indulgent life, I disqualify myself from heart-to-heart fellowship with Christ and hold back guidance. If I obey the instructions in God's Word, I will find God's Will, if I disregard them, I won't. Ninety per cent of knowing God's Will is, of course, being willing to do it before I even know what it is!

2. THERE ARE LIMITS TO OBSERVE

If I deliberately step beyond the limits God puts down in His Word for me, I will stray from His Will. The Lord Jesus said that the Christian walk would take us on what He described as a "narrow way." That narrow way does not get any wider the longer I am on it, does it? It will be narrow right to the end. There will be kerb-stones and fences, limits set to where I can walk. The "broad way", on the other hand, "which leads to destruction", has not got the same limits. On the broad way I can by and large say what I like, think what I like, behave how I like and, I can carry what baggage I like. The choice is mine. If I want to walk the narrow way which leads to life, I must observe the limits it sets.

3. THERE ARE EXAMPLES TO FOLLOW

There is nothing quite like Scripture to show me examples of men and women finding and doing God's Will in their lives. From the butler Nehemiah to the gleaner, Ruth; from the shepherd boy David to the fig-picker, Amos; from the intellectual Daniel to the little servant girl in the house of Naaman; from the garment-making Dorcas to the tent-making Paul, all found God's guidance and did His Will. You and I can follow their example.

4. THERE IS WISDOM TO DRAW ON

I refer, in part, to the book of Proverbs. This book has a lot to say about the issues of life. Here is instruction for young people in a world where subtle and restless efforts are made to poison their hearts and pervert their ways. Here are verbal gold vaults of wisdom for parents raising a family. Here are words of advice for those who are unemployed and living from hand to mouth. Here is incisive warning about the power of speech. Here you will read wisdom regarding anger, education, food, drink, justice, greed, self-control, the place of a woman and the place of a man in society and much more.

To sum up our Biblical approach to guidance, here are ten checkpoints to help when we are seeking God's Will in any situation;

1. Ask the question; "What is the best I can do for my God in this situation?".
2. Note the instructions of Scripture; on many issues the Bible has already spoken.
3. Follow the examples of Godliness in Scripture. Imitate the love and humility of Jesus Himself.
4. Let wisdom judge the best course of action; the question we should ask is no longer; "What is God's Will?"; instead the question is; "How do I make good decisions?"
5. Always note nudges from God that come your way; special burdens of concern or restlessness of heart might indicate that something needs to be changed.
6. Cherish the Divine peace that Paul says, "garrisons" the hearts of those who are in God's Will.

7. Observe the limits set by circumstances to what is possible. When it is clear those limits cannot be changed, accept them as from God.
8. Be prepared for God's guidance to be withheld until the right time comes for a decision. God usually guides one step at a time.
9. Be prepared for God to direct you to something you do not like, and teach you to like it!
10. Never forget that if you make a bad decision, it is not the end. God forgives and restores.

We have come a long way in this book from Napoleon's ignoring of the message given when the storks flew South. We return, though, to their message. The Scriptures are fascinating in that they mock and rebuke people when they fail to do by their minds and consent what animals do by instinct. They tell us to go to the ant and consider her ways and be wise. This little creature is prudent and industrious by instinct and often, with all our human understanding, we are not. The oxen and donkey we are told give their masters a more obedient recognition than people give to God their Creator.

It is to Jeremiah, though, that we turn as we close this book. A heartbroken prophet with a heartbreaking message, Jeremiah laboured more than forty years to proclaim a message to the stiff-necked people of Judah. Despised and persecuted by his countrymen, Jeremiah bathed his harsh prophecies in tears of compassion. Through all of his sermons and signs, he faithfully declared that surrender to God's will is the only way to escape calamity. No-one has ever put such a truth more hauntingly than Jeremiah when he wrote, "Even the stork in the heavens knows her appointed time; and the turtle dove, the swift, and the swallow observe the time of their coming. But my people do not know the judgment of the Lord."

When human beings fail to do by consent and mind what animals do by instinct they are contradicting themselves. They are contradicting their creation and their distinctive humanity and are missing God's best in their lives. The message of the storks who flew South still signals a warning to us. Let's heed it.

Bibliography

"Napoleon", Vincent Cronin (Collins 1971)

"Lincoln at Gettysburg", Gary Willis (Simon and Schuster, 1992)

"Lincoln", B. J. Thomas (Eyre and Spotiswoode, 1953)

"Kill Devil Hill," Harry B. Combs with Marlin Cardin (Secker and Warburg, 1980)

"Wilbur and Orville", Fred Howard (Robert Hale, 1988)

"The ship that stood still", Leslie Read (Patrick Stephens Ltd, 1993)

"The night lives on," Walter Lord (Viking, 1980)

"'The Titanic", the full story of a tragedy," Michael Davie (Bodley Head, London, 1986)

"'Alexander Fleming' - the man and the myth", Gwyn MacFarlane (Chatto and Windus; The Hogarth Press, London, 1984)

"The life of Sir Alexander Fleming," Andre Marrois (Jonathan Cape Ltd, 1959)

"Hitler and the Jews; the genesis of the Holocaust," Phillippe Burren (Edward Arnold, 1994)

"Children with a star", Deborah Dwork (Yale University Press, 1991)

"Mrs Browning: the story of Elizabeth Barrett", Rosealine Mander (Weidenfield and Nicolson, London, 1980)

"Robert Browning: a life within a life", Donald Thomas (Weidenfield and Nicolson, London, 1982)

"Pontious Pilate", Paul L. Maier, (Living Books, Tyndale House Publishers, Inc. Wheaton, Illinois, 1968)

"The Gospel of John," William Barclay, (The Daily Bible Study, Saint Andrew Press)

"The Gospel According to John", G. Cambell Morgan (Marshall, Morgan and Scott Ltd. London, 1946)

***

• Material from "The Holocaust" by Martin Gilbert and published by Harper Collins Publishers Limited, namely the testimony of Franciszek Zabecki, eye witness at Treblinka Station (p. 398-400) and the testimony of Rudolf Reder, a survivor of Belzec Camp (p. 413-417) is used by kind permission.